UNLEARNING WITH HANNAH ARENDT

UNLEARNING WITH HANNAH ARENDT

MARIE LUISE KNOTT

TRANSLATED FROM THE GERMAN
BY DAVID DOLLENMAYER

OTHER PRESS
NEW YORK

Copyright © 2011 MSB Matthes & Seitz Berlin Verlagsgesellschaft mbH
All rights reserved by and controlled through Matthes & Seitz Verlag Berlin.
Originally published in German as *Verlernen: Denkwege bei Hannah Arendt*
by Matthes & Seitz Berlin in 2011.

Translation copyright © 2013 by David Dollenmayer

The translation of this work was funded by Geisteswissenschaften International,
Translation Funding for Humanities and Social Sciences from Germany, a joint
initiative of the Fritz Thyssen Foundation, the German Federal Foreign Office,
the collecting society VG WORT, and the Börsenverein des Deutschen Buchhandels
(German Publishers & Booksellers Association).

Excerpts from *Essays in Understanding, 1930–1954* by Hannah Arendt. Copyright
© 1994 by Hannah Arendt. Reprinted by permission of Georges Borchardt, Inc.,
on behalf of the Hannah Arendt Bluecher Literary Trust. Excerpts from *The Human
Condition* by Hannah Arendt. Copyright © 1958 by The University of Chicago.
Reprinted by permission of the University of Chicago Press.

Excerpt from "Where Are the War Poets" by Cecil Day Lewis, from *The Complete
Poems of C. Day Lewis*, Stanford University Press, 1992. Copyright © 1992 The Estate
of C. Day Lewis. Reprinted by permission of SLL/Sterling Lord Literistic, Inc.

Illustrations by Nanne Meyer

Production Editor: Yvonne E. Cárdenas

Text Designer: Julie Fry

This book was set in Swift and Benton Sans

10 9 8 7 6 5 4 3 2 1

Library of Congress Cataloging-in-Publication Data

Knott, Marie Luise.
    [Verlernen. English]
    Unlearning with Hannah Arendt / by Marie Luise Knott ; translated
from the German by David Dollenmayer ; illustrations by Nanne Meyer.
    pages cm
    Includes bibliographical references.
    ISBN 978-1-59051-647-8 (hardcover) — ISBN 978-1-59051-648-5 (e-book)
    1. Arendt, Hannah, 1906–1975. I. Meyer, Nanne, 1953– II. Title.
    B945.A694K6613 2014
    191—dc23
                                                2013047205

FOR M.W.

CONTENTS

PREFACE

> *When someday this long affliction*
> *will have broken up, like ice,*
> *it will be spoken of*
> *as of the Black Death;*
> *and children on the heath*
> *will build a man of straw*
> *to burn delight from suffering*
> *and light from ancient dread.*
> —Gottfried Keller[1]

"I never doubted that there must be someone like you, but now you actually exist and my extraordinary joy at that fact will last forever." Thus wrote the poet and novelist Ingeborg Bachmann after meeting Hannah Arendt in New York. It was a meeting of kindred spirits. "How beautiful the last novella was with its great love," Arendt later wrote to the novelist Uwe Johnson after Bachmann's death.

In "Three Paths to the Lake,"[2] the novella to which Arendt refers, the photojournalist Elisabeth Matrei attempts to reach the lake of her childhood by many more than just three paths. She seeks to recover beauty, serenity, and a (vanished) familiar world. But she comes to the realization that one generation no longer holds out a hand to the next. The paths of her childhood are passé. All of them must be newly reconnoitered and traveled for their own sake. The same is true of love, Bachmann's starting point and secret motivation. Love flares up whether impracticable or not. And although it may fail, it is inexhaustible.

The thought paths in the work of Hannah Arendt traced in the following chapters resemble Elisabeth Matrei's real and metaphoric pathways. They all follow from the shock of the twentieth century: the realization that National Socialism was a force that threatened to completely redefine the essence of being human. Arendt quotes W. H. Auden:

All words like Peace and Love,
All sane affirmative speech,
Had been soiled, profaned, debased
To a horrid mechanical screech.

National Socialism attempted to force people into its own monocausal, "logical" linguistic system with rigidly fixed images, to fetter them with the definitions of a totalitarian structure. All talk of the good, the true, and the beautiful (Auden's "Peace and Love") was degraded and defiled, drowned out by a "horrid mechanical screech." How could one escape such ensnaring prejudices and come into possession of one's own language for what had been seen and heard and done? Arendt the theoretician found in Gottfried Keller's poem an image for the need to "unlearn" the familiar and make it again unknown.[3] She felt that the poet said it better than she could: "To burn delight from suffering and light from ancient dread."

All four chapters of this book—on laughter, translation, forgiveness, and dramatization—are inquiries into how Hannah Arendt awakens delight from suffering and light from ancient dread. They mark out escape routes from the dead ends of existing traditional conceptions of the world and the human being. These pathways are like lumbermen's forest roads: temporary, ad hoc, and liable to end abruptly. Their intent is not to found a new school of thought but to cultivate the existing forest, to recapture a world under threat. Walter Benjamin formulated it this way in a review of stories by Oskar Maria Graf: "We seldom think about how much freedom it takes to tell even the smallest story. Any bias robs the narrator of a bit of his articulateness"[4]—and thus of some bit of his world, one might add.

This book is about breaking loose from such bias and the territory of freedom gained thereby. The pathways of thought we will sketch have need of poetry, which in its nakedness and directness invades analytic language and allows it to open up; Arendt rejects instruments of comprehension that have proved dull or irrelevant. She allows them to go missing, unlearns them. Many things must be freed from entanglements so that we can argue about and conquer them anew. Such acts of "unlearning," born of shock and distress, are intellectual awakenings. The paralyzing horror of encountering Adolf Eichmann is interrupted by *laughter*. Through the intellectual activity of *translation*, the misery of the immigrant is transformed into the "insouciance of a pariah."[5] Not as enmeshed in the social realities of her new country as she was in the old one, she can allow her gaze wider scope to roam. The unlearning that is *forgiveness* is—*pars pro toto*—a desperate struggle to drive out of one's head images and concepts whose traditional significance inhibits thought. And by means of *dramatization*, the text itself becomes a stage, a secure space where people under threat of becoming marionettes controlled by social conventions can discover their "human distinctness."[6]

––––––

Studies of Hannah Arendt as a political theoretician were only marginal to my motivation for editing a collection of her essays in 1986.[7] At the time, I was unsettled by the results of her thinking, but even more by Arendt's ability to allow the reality she encountered to shake and confuse her. Her eloquent writings brought fresh wind to the act of thinking, a wind that was perhaps a result of the peculiar tension between the pariah's distance from society and the citizen's duty to intervene and even to commit principled acts of civil disobedience. Her rejection of philosophy, which sounded so final in 1933 ("Never again! I shall never again get involved in any kind of intellectual business"[8]), her well-founded mistrust of everything that she thought she knew but that had been unable to stand up to reality, was articulated in her texts and awakened my interest. Here was someone who was seeking a new pact between language and life. Her texts were about how all events and facts, by their very existence, place a demand on our intellectual attention, even though she knew that in everyday life we don't always have the strength, time, or inclination to respond to that demand, to pause and think.

Unlike the "unlearning" Barbara Hahn refers to in her work on Hannah Arendt,[9] the unlearning that runs through this book cannot be imposed upon the self, nor can it be learned. The four pathways of thought I will mark out are not the products of any plan. Instead, they are re-actions to the shock of what is purely factual. The acts of laughing, translating, forgiving, and dramatizing keep open the rift caused by that shock and keep us moving in relation to that rift.

Among the new impulses in the reception of Hannah Arendt's work that let us feel more of that fresh wind mentioned above, the publication of the *Denktagebuch* (Intellectual diary) must be mentioned first of all, followed by the books, essays, and collections of Barbara Hahn, Wolfgang Heuer, Ingeborg Nordmann, and Thomas Wild. My own close collaboration with Barbara Hahn as joint curators of an exhibition in 2006 as well as the unexpected material we discovered then have found their way into the present work.[10]

———

A basic experience underlying this book is that Arendt's texts are inexhaustible; they unfold more and more with each new reading. One suspects that as our present becomes ever more distant from the historical circumstances that originally gave rise to her thought, Arendt's works will turn out to have new and quite different things to say to us. For each generation they hold in store (to stick to the metaphor of our epigraph) new delight and light, the delight of action and deliberation as well as a bright store of questions and images. The power of her images and concepts creates a safe place where readers can feel confident of being involved in essential intellectual processes—even in the midst of their own perplexity.

UNLEARNING WITH HANNAH ARENDT

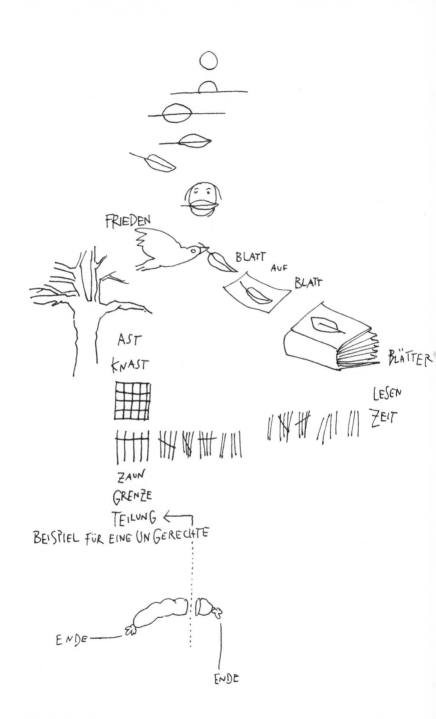

FRIEDEN

BLATT AUF BLATT

BLÄTTER

LESEN

ZEIT

AST
KNAST

ZAUN
GRENZE
TEILUNG ←
BEISPIEL FÜR EINE UNGERECHTE

ENDE —

ENDE

LAUGHTER:
THE SUDDEN TURN OF THE MIND

Hearing the speeches that ring from your house, one laughs.
But whoever sees you, reaches for his knife.
—Bertolt Brecht[1]

Because of her laughter, Hannah Arendt was subject to fierce attacks from all over the world and virtual "excommunication"[2] from the Jewish people after publication of her report on the Eichmann trial in 1963. What provoked her laughter were the transcripts of interrogations of the former SS Obersturmbann-führer Adolf Eichmann. As director of the National Socialist government's office of Jewish affairs and evacuation, he had organized the deportations to the death camps. After the war, Eichmann lived under a false name in Argentina until 1960, when the Mossad, the Israeli intelligence service, abducted him to Jerusalem to stand trial for crimes against the Jewish people and crimes against humanity. Prior to his trial, he had been described as "a perverted, sadistic personality"[3] and a fanatical anti-Semite who, it was said, combined an "insatiable urge to kill"[4] with implacable devotion to duty. It was this same Nazi perpetrator, wearing a suit and sitting in a glass booth, whom Hannah Arendt labeled a "random buffoon"[5] and who on his own had acquired for himself neither purpose nor orientation in life. His acts were monstrous,

A key to the text in the illustrations begins on page 169.

but their perpetrator seemed to her all too ordinary and average. Arendt described him thus: "Eichmann was no Iago and no Macbeth, and nothing was further from his mind than to decide to become a villain like Richard III. He had no motives at all except an unusual assiduousness to do anything to further his career, and even this assiduousness was not criminal; he would certainly never have murdered his superior in order to replace him. To express it in plain language, he simply had *never imagined what effect his actions had.*"[6]

———

Arendt was eager to go to Jerusalem in 1961 and report on the trial for *The New Yorker*. At a time when the crimes committed by the Nazis threatened to exceed the statute of limitations in Germany, many burning questions remained unanswered. How were Eichmann's deeds to be prosecuted? How could one try him for crimes for which no commensurate punishment existed? And how could so many other perpetrators have escaped punishment? Which institutions had the will and the jurisdiction to prosecute these crimes? Most of the higher judgeships in the Federal Republic of Germany, after all, were held by former Nazis. Did an Israeli court have the authority to try crimes against the Jewish people even though they had been committed before the state of Israel was even founded and in locations that did not lie within its present borders?

An additional factor was that Hannah Arendt knew about the Nuremberg Trials only from newspaper reports and what she had been told by friends who were present at the international military tribunal in 1945. She wanted to attend the trial of a Nazi perpetrator herself and observe such a man in person.

Hannah Arendt was already well known when she went to Israel in 1961. She was an American citizen and a champion of civil rights who criticized Israel's nonsecular society with its two categories of citizenship. She was a former German who in 1933 had escaped Germany's methodical destruction of the Jews and who expected to encounter a monster in Eichmann but instead found "thoughtlessness," that is, absence of thought.[7] And she was a Jew who had advocated an all-Jewish army to fight against Hitler but was outraged during the trial by the prosecutor's questioning of survivors. Arendt found the question "Why didn't you revolt and charge and attack?"[8] "cruel and silly."[9] Cruel because it thrust the witnesses back into the powerlessness they had experienced, and silly because in the trial, the question and its answer predicated that history had *necessarily* taken place in this way and not another.

———

In 1963, Hannah Arendt's report on the Eichmann trial appeared first as a series of articles in *The New Yorker* and that same year as a book. It caused a scandal, and not just among Jews. Arendt criticized the conduct of the trial but approved of the death sentence. Gershom Scholem accused her of downplaying Nazi crimes. Many people were outraged to hear them described as banal. Jewish authorities were especially offended by the following widely quoted sentence: "The whole truth was that if the Jewish people had really been unorganized and leaderless, there would have been chaos and plenty of misery but the total number of victims would hardly have been between four and a half and six million people."[10] According to Scholem, Arendt was thereby suggesting that Jews somehow bore a measure of responsibility for the Holocaust.[11]

This is not the place to examine in detail the differences of opinion and misunderstandings on both sides, or whether the book actually caused such a stir because it represented, as Karl Jaspers put it in a letter to Arendt at the time, an "act of aggression against 'life-sustaining lies.'"[12] It must also remain an open question whether Eichmann's testimony in Jerusalem was merely an act that Arendt allowed herself to be fooled by. Nor shall I discuss whether Arendt was right that during the war, there would have been other possible courses of action for the Jewish authorities. In her report, Arendt, the theoretician of political action, was concerned with preserving the human capacity to act. She asked herself whether there are times under a totalitarian regime when the refusal to act becomes itself an action. Based on the testimony during the trial, she also asked if it was possible—or even imperative—to reassess whether disbanding Jewish representative bodies after 1941 and thereby creating a (rebellious) dispersion of Jewish leadership would have had any effect at all.[13]

Today, even more than in the atmosphere of 1963, it is also obvious how much Arendt was concerned with the fate of Israel. "I'm toying with the idea of a second motto: 'How badly protected is Israel? False friends guard her gates from without and foolishness and fear reign within'—from memory, from Heine's *Rabbi von Bacharach*. What do you think?" she wrote to the publisher Klaus Piper on April 6, 1964.[14] In contrast, Arendt assumed that during the war "nothing would have helped but a 'normalization' of the Jewish position, that is, a real declaration of war, the establishment of a Jewish army, composed of Palestinian and stateless Jews all over the world, and the recognition of the Jewish people as belligerents."[15] But for a prosecution to have its witnesses constantly testifying that there was nothing they could have done or achieved was to call into question man's basic capacity to act. In the person of Eichmann, Arendt saw this capacity threatened in a completely different way. In a 1964 television interview with the German historian Joachim Fest, she said,

> I want to talk about Eichmann, since I'm familiar with him. The first thing to be said is the following. You see, collective action—collective action, where many act together—generates power. You are never powerful when you act alone, no matter how strong you are. The feeling of power generated by acting together is in and of itself absolutely not evil. It's a normal human trait. But it's not good, either. It's simply neutral, something that is simply a phenomenon, a phenomenon of being human that must be described as such. There is a pronounced feeling of pleasure involved in such action. I'm not going to start quoting you examples—I could go on for hours just with examples from the American Revolution. And I would now say that the real perversion of action is functioning; that the feeling of pleasure is still present in such functioning; but that everything that is present in action, including communal action—namely, we confer with one another, we arrive at certain decisions, we accept responsibility, we think about what we're doing—that all that is switched off in functioning. You have here an example of pure function without a goal, a running in neutral. And the pleasure in pure function—that pleasure was quite evident in the case of Eichmann.[16]

Many readers of *Eichmann in Jerusalem* did not understand how dangerous Arendt considered the "pleasure in pure function." Arendt was attacked first and foremost for her ironic tone.

She described Eichmann as she found him: a mass murderer without motive who murdered as a part of his career.[17] The insight that the Nazi criminals were not demons but human beings was a basic cause of confusion. But the Eichmann whom Hannah Arendt encountered at the trial corresponded to none of her expectations. He confused her, and she allowed herself to be confused. She found a person who claimed under interrogation that he had never had evil or murderous intentions, an SS leader and organizer of the Holocaust who could both regret that he was not able to complete his assignment to kill eleven million Jews and say of himself in a chatty tone that, instead of anti-Semitism, he had a feeling in his heart for Jews since reading Theodor Herzl's *The Jewish State*, and had always believed in the necessity of such a state. In one passage of her report, after Eichmann's testimony in which he suggested to Heydrich that the way to fulfill the latter's promise to make Bohemia and Moravia *judenrein* (cleansed of Jews) was to concentrate the dispersed Jews into a special area, Arendt adds between ironic parentheses "(A Jewish homeland, a gathering-in of the exiles in the Diaspora)."[18] Of course she didn't mean for her readers to take this Zionist vocabulary seriously when applied to one of the men principally responsible for the destruction of the Jews. She was only trying to put into words the completely unexpected, mindless absurdity she encountered in the person of Eichmann—put it into words rather than fall silent.

Where the horror was blackest and the confusion deepest, she resorted to "*burschikose Ironie*" (irrepressible irony), which she described to Joachim Fest as "my most precious inheritance from Germany—or more precisely, from Berlin." Old friends abandoned her. When Gershom Scholem wrote to her, "I would just like to say that your portrait of Eichmann as a convert to Zionism is only conceivable from someone with your deep resentment of everything having to do with Zionism,"[19] she answered, "I never made Eichmann out to be a 'Zionist.' If you missed the irony of the sentence—which was plainly in *oratio obliqua* reporting Eichmann's own words—I really can't help it."[20]

Irony is her means of holding experience at arm's length in order to think it through, a protection against panic and powerfully aggressive impulses that would only interfere with her ability to judge.

———

Moreover, behind the tone of the Eichmann book lies a quite real laughter that overcame Arendt as she read the transcripts of his interrogation, "I'll tell you this: I read the transcript of his police investigation, thirty-six hundred pages, read it, and read it carefully, and I do not know how many times I laughed—laughed out loud! People took this reaction in a bad way. I cannot do anything about that. But I know one thing: Three minutes before certain death, I probably still would laugh."[21] As a test, she had taken at face value what she saw and what Eichmann said about himself: nothing but clichés whose "thoughtlessness" so shocked her that she burst out laughing, thereby outraging not only the Jewish world.

CONFIDENCE IN MANKIND

Philosophers, poets, and scientists often say that their most important discoveries come to them as sudden insights. Arendt owed her insight into the "banality of evil,"[22] an idea that would in the end ring in a whole new era in her life's work, at least partly to laughter—her laughter over Eichmann's "thought-lessness." What should one think of the laughter in Hannah Arendt's work?

Spontaneous laughter is a reaction that bypasses reason and can potentially give momentum to freedom and sovereignty in the midst of the constraints of this world and all its buttoned-up social conventions. Laughter, which is most often generated in interaction with others, has the ability to lighten life's grimmer moments. It can disentangle us: "The friend of the oppressed will always need that great confidence in our fellow men which teaches us to laugh."[23] Laughter teaches something that in 1942, at the height of the Second World War when the preceding sentence was written, was not to be found in seriousness, that is, by calling upon sense and reason. Laughter makes available confidence in our fellow man, confidence in the human power of resistance—against ideology and terror, against obscurantism, repression, dogmatism, and despotism. As Walter Benjamin, who taught Arendt much about life's contradictions and dead ends, said, "Let me note in passing that there is no better starting place for thought than in laughter. Specifically, the convulsion of the diaphragm usually offers better opportunities for thought than the convulsion of the soul."[24]

In 1943, amid horrifying news from Europe, Arendt again reflected on the liberating power of laughter to transcend reality. The occasion was an article on Franz Kafka, the master of fear. Implicitly in opposition to the thesis that Kafka foresaw National Socialism, she wrote that no work of the imagination could any longer compete with present reality.[25] Kafka's stories, she wrote, had left behind the helplessness of the living, and his figures, without the time or opportunity to develop individual characteristics, were all constructs of gigantic and comical exaggeration, so indescribably amusing that they can almost console us for our real-life disappointments. For in Kafka's texts, laughter is "a humorous excitement that permits man to prove his essential freedom through a kind of serene superiority to his own failures,"[26] if only because he can think of something that transgresses the boundaries of reality. In laughter, we transgress rationally comprehensible reality. But to what end?

———

The wisdom of children and the imagination of poets and novelists are both able to displace things, to move them somewhere else. Laughter has a similar effect, as Arendt asserts when she writes that in the alternative world it evokes, the mysterious powers of reality so thoroughly described by Kafka lose their power—if only for the moment of laughter. In Kafka's fiction, laughter is the answer of the human being who knows that even though he, like all people, is bound to die, he does not have to be, nor is he, a cog in a machine, a flunky carrying out alien laws. Even in the darkest times, these moments of laughter can give humankind and humaneness strength over those laws. And she wrote that in 1943.

That same year, the essay "We Refugees"—from start to finish a treatise of the most bitter irony—appeared in the American Jewish periodical the *Menorah Journal*. She tells of a lonely émigré dachshund who in his grief dreams of lost greatness, "Once, when I was a Saint Bernhard..."[27] There is hardly another image that expresses so succinctly the wrenching dislocations and loss of one's reality and home ground that are the refugee's lot.

Arendt's critique of her own former hope of assimilation is bitterly sharp:

> Our optimism, indeed, is admirable, even if we say so ourselves. The story of our struggle has finally become known. We lost our home, which means the familiarity of daily life. We lost our occupation, which means the confidence that we are of some use in the world. We lost our language, which means the naturalness of reactions, the simplicity of gestures, the unaffected expression of feelings. We left our relatives in the Polish ghettos and our best friends have been killed in concentration camps, and that means the rupture of our private lives.
>
> Nevertheless, as soon as we were saved—and most of us had to be saved several times—we started our new lives and tried to follow as closely as possible all the good advice our saviours passed on to us. We were told to forget; and we forgot quicker than anybody ever could imagine. In a friendly way we were reminded that the new country would become a new home, and after four weeks in France or six weeks in America, we pretended to be Frenchmen or Americans. The more optimistic among us would even add that their whole former life had been passed in a kind of unconscious exile and only their new country now taught them what a home really looks like.[28]

The essay revealed and dramatized how thin the ice was on which every refugee walked, at least every refugee who was nothing but a Jew and refused to take up arms as a Jew. If the refugee, who after all was a creature of flesh and blood and not simply an abstraction, was not to break through that thin ice, laughter would outfit him with a necessary eerie lightness.

THE HANNAH BOOK

Among Karl Jaspers's literary remains there are several cartons labeled "Hannah-Buch"—a manuscript he never completed.[29] Arendt's dissertation adviser and dear friend Jaspers, whom she once described as the "embodiment of freedom, reason, and communication,"[30] had completed versions of some chapters; others were still in the planning stage. Jaspers was motivated to write the book by his outrage at the defamation of Arendt because of her Eichmann report. Jaspers praised Arendt's "tone of veracity," her "determination to be truthful in her view of humanity." He had no intention of countering the accusations against her point by point. He was indignant at their baselessness, especially since in his opinion, her attackers "simply ignored" the content of the book. Jaspers wanted to use the Eichmann story to explore the meaning of the "dependencies" of our thinking and, at the same time, work out the distinguishing features of Arendt's "independence of thought"—even when, as Jaspers noted, a shadow lay across her texts, the "shadow of runaway horses"—that is, her allowing herself to get carried away. He saw Arendt in the same light as Rosa Luxemburg and John F. Kennedy. As a counterexample, he noted Bismarck. In a section titled "Interrogating Hannah's Thought in the Realm of Research and Philosophy" there is a folder on "Her Laughter and Irony." It contains notations such as, "She lives in the belief that there is something humane deeply ingrained and indestructible within man .... For her, nothing tangible is final. For anything that is tangible is limited and deprived of freedom if one takes it for more." In another passage, "She thinks her way into what is inconceivable; she knows no peace."

As much as Arendt probably welcomed any support during the massive and at times concerted attacks against her Eichmann book, Jaspers's plan made her uncomfortable. Although she provided him with material, she was relieved that the book was never completed. In his draft foreword, Jaspers expresses his relief that the planned character assassination had not been succesful. Arendt had emerged "from the affair as a pure, serious, independent thinker." "She was offered positions at American universities, received honorary doctorates, the Library of Congress established a Hannah Arendt Archive."

It is no surprise that Jaspers intended to write a separate chapter not just on Arendt's ironic tone but also on her laughter, for laughter played an important role in their relationship. Jaspers describes their shared laughter thus: "Everything that presents itself as solemn, weighty, and pretentious in today's world becomes the object of her laughter, and thus the bearers of this solemnity find Hannah Arendt unbearable. The whole world of George, for example...is for her nothing but an object of laughter except for a few outstanding poems, especially from George's earlier years, and the important scholarly accomplishments of some of his followers such as Kantorowicz."[31]

This is a liberating laughter; it creates freedom and connection, gives substantive differences their due and keeps them in flux.[32] When the partners in a debate concentrate only on their differences, identifying and insisting on them, they are emphasizing what divides them, thereby letting the divide grow wider, gain significance, and become more palpable. By contrast, laughter builds bridges. Emotionalism looses its edge in laughter; difference and the experience of it are allowed to float free and feel secure in that hovering state. We are bitterly in need of laughter as an all too rare bridge between groups of people, a bridge that both connects them and maintains their distance from one another.

With Hannah Arendt, Jaspers shared a different laughter from the laughter of irony. About the ironic tone of *Eichmann in Jerusalem*, he wrote, "Laughter runs through the book, the quiet laughter (of irony) that allows what is comical to be acknowledged in order to make what is serious palpable—a powerful, liberating laughter that discerns the comical in what is so shameful, when instead of the temple we expected...we find only inanity." The location of insight could not be sought in seriousness, that is, under the requirements of sense and reason, through analytic thought. Upon serious consideration by a thinking person, it is unimaginable that someone like Eichmann could say in his own defense, "Where would we end up if everyone would have his own thoughts?"[33] Something in the act of thinking blocks our access to this kind of seriousness. Laughter, on the other hand, makes it possible for our intellect to regain access to seriousness from another dimension.

EICHMANN AND "IRREPRESIBLE IRONY"

In 1963, Arendt was accused of adopting the wrong tone, of being inappropriately ironic. In the opinion of her critics, irony was a faux pas that betrayed her lack of "Ahavat Yisrael"—love of the Jewish people—in the words of Gershom Scholem. Irony as a rhetorical device had long had a negative connotation. A "way of speaking that expresses content through its opposite in conjunction with an expressive emphasis or attitude" was regarded by many as devious and dishonest. That began to change at the latest with Friederich Schlegel's insight that irony was useful when one "was aware of the limits of what can be expressed."[34] Schlegel appreciated the value of irony as a stylistic device and recognized its riskiness as well. Irony requires, on the one hand, rhetorical signals, and on the other, people capable of receiving and understanding them. In all ironic seriousness, Heinrich Heine is supposed to have suggested that someone ought to introduce an irony point for German, on the model of the exclamation point. When the Jew Hannah Arendt called the Jew-murderer Eichmann a Zionist, such an irony point might have done wonders.

Arendt's writing is characterized by "a deeper urge to get to the truth of things than the rest of us [have]," as her friend J. Glenn Gray, the philosopher and translator of Heidegger, wrote to her after reading the Eichmann report.[35] Karl Jaspers had planned to write a chapter on laughter because he knew that Arendt's laughter was part of this "deeper urge to get to the truth of things." When one reads the documentary evidence of the debate today, one can still feel what a bold act the Eichmann book must have represented in its day and what drama it must have caused.

The image of barbaric murderers, motivated by profound anti-Semitism, was all too plausible and, at the same time, practical. It was hard to part with the idea that the Nazis were radically evil, as Arendt herself had still assumed in *The Origins of Totalitarianism*. Although we are philosophically unable to conceive of "radical evil," Arendt wrote, "in their effort to prove that everything is possible, totalitarian regimes have discovered without knowing it that there are crimes which men can neither punish nor forgive."[36] The death camps had "the appearance of some radical evil previously unknown to us."[37]

Postwar Germans, who wanted to regard themselves as good people, could live more easily with the image of radically evil Nazis. The perpetrators, the Germans who had transported Jews to concentration camps and then murdered them, were the evil people, the others! The Germans themselves were not monsters. For the Jews, too, it was seductively easy to hang on to the image of omnipotent and evil Nazis. In the end, it is easier to think of yourself and your people as the victims of "the devil in human disguise" than as the victims of a "some average man on the street."[38]

Received wisdom and the emotional tone in which people usually broached this subject did not accord with Arendt's observations. In their correspondence with Arendt and published reviews of her work, writers such as Rosalie L. Colie, Mary McCarthy, and Robert Lowell recognized the novelty and independence of her perspective. They emphasized that Arendt had avoided both the danger of what Lowell called "concentration camp sentimentalism" and the traditional Romantic concept of evil. Sentimentalism and Romanticism were means of suspending thought at a time when the last thing that was needed was to minimize the enormity of events or drown thought in clichés. As Reinhart Baumgart wrote, "What she is trying to grasp in the policy of extermination is not what is simply a continuation of the past, but rather what it heralds as a possible model for the future."[39] Her encounter with this earnest man who uttered nothing but clichés and speech balloons during his interrogations and was in fact coresponsible for the death of millions of Jews, this man who was an SS leader and organizer of the Holocaust, an anti-Semite who claimed to be a philo-Zionist, this human phenomenon of the gravest importance who had such a vulgar air about him—the encounter tested the limits of what can be expressed. The shock was profound. Here was something totally new, something completely unexpected. There existed no way to think about it.

Obviously, Arendt was unable to write a soberly analytical report about what she had seen and heard. Irony was a means to keep the fear the phenomenon evoked at arm's length. The question remained how that fear could make what Jaspers called "*der Sprung zur Ruhe*"—the leap to serenity.

Arendt's distress—questions, answers, hesitations, and new questions—found its way into her reportage. She allowed her readers to participate in her confusion, and that became part of the character of the book. The challenge of having to confront what had been done and the challenge of her tone are perhaps more closely connected than has often been recognized. When Arendt ignored conventional moral judgments (including her own) and set out to suspend the conventional hatred of Eichmann (including her own) and allow herself to be touched by what she saw and heard, when she thus cast aside her bearings, readers lost their bearings as well, their sense of which feelings were appropriate. They were as disoriented as she was. That is indeed the great challenge. If the image of radical evil did not apply, then imagination—both the author's and the reader's—was called for.

THOUGHT CATCHES ITS BREATH

Critics have often interpreted Arendt's Eichmann-laughter as haughty and arrogant, and this charge is not without justification. There are two sides to laughter. A laugher is clearing space for a shared sound, but he is also showing what Homer called the "fence of his teeth." Such aggression is always aimed not just at others, but at one's own weakness as well—the temptation to remain within the bounds of traditional thought or of what one already knows or has learned. Arendt's laughter was the laughter of incongruence, the laughter that erupts when facing absurdity, a pause to catch one's intellectual breath. We happen upon something that makes no sense, we laugh, and respond with wit.[40] For while laughter is a re-action, irony and wit are (spoken or written) actions. Irony expresses the unwillingness or the inability to put up with nonsense.

Wit arises when people can easily and quickly see similarities between dissimilar things. They have at their command a peculiar and unteachable skill that Kant called *Verähnlichungsvermögen*, a "similarity-creating ability" with regard to phenomena "that often are quite distant from each other according to the laws of association."[41] The laughter of a person with wit thus creates bridges between distant things—similar to metaphor, which Federico García Lorca has called "a steeple-chase jump of the imagination."[42] In a letter to Benno von Wiese, Arendt wrote engagingly but also a bit aggressively, "When you write 'we succumbed to the spirit of the times,' it sounds very nice as long as one forgets that Hitler, who looked like a con artist and not like a Napoleon, was the embodiment of that spirit."[43]

In creating similarities, both wit and metaphor bridge intellectual and interpersonal abysses and establish a new coherence in the world. As a performative act, moreover, wit is intent upon getting others to laugh, too. Hannah Arendt can be heard giving just such a bridging laugh in the face of the incompatible in 1964, when the journalist and diplomat Günter Gaus invited her to a televised conversation as part of a series called *Zur Person* (Personal details). The topic was to be Arendt's life and work. It is an interview that still astonishes. Arendt smokes one cigarette after another, and you get the feeling you are seeing and hearing her think. In one passage, she discusses the excruciating experience of watching her intellectual friends become *gleichgeschaltet*—engaged in National Socialism in 1933. She speaks of the emptiness that opened up around her. Thirty years after leaving Germany, Arendt was still unable to come to grips with this experience in complete sentences. Words still failed her:

> Among intellectuals Gleichschaltung was the rule, so to speak. But [*Here she hesitates and speaks very slowly.*] not...among...the others. [*Here her voice trails off. Then it rises again and regains its strength. Her train of thought can continue.*].... No one ever blamed someone if he "co-ordinated" because he had to take care of his family. The worst thing was that they really believed in Nazism! For a short time, some for a very short time. But that means that they made up ideas about Hitler [*She chuckles.*], in part terrifically interesting things! Completely fantastic and interesting and complicated things! [*Her voice cracks with laughter.*] Things far above the ordinary level! [*Arendt, who usually spoke quickly and coherently, cannot control her bizarre laughter while talking about this. Then she finds her way back to fluent speech.*] I found that grotesque. Today I would say that they were trapped by their own ideas.[44]

Thirty years later, she has to laugh when recalling the experience, for example, Benno von Wiese paying her a visit in Berlin and exclaiming, "What great times we live in!" Or Martin Heidegger, in his inaugural speech on becoming rector of Freiburg University, celebrating "the greatness, the honorableness of this national awakening" and—by drawing upon Plato's three classes of producers, soldiers, and rulers—glorifying National Socialism as a triad of "labor service," "military service" and "knowledge service."[45] It could have been hysterically funny if it hadn't been so deadly earnest.

THE SALUBRIOUS MOVEMENT OF THE DIAPHRAGM

Laughter, what Immanuel Kant called the "salubrious movement of the diaphragm," is physically dependent on the ability to let go. In letting go, we create a transgression, a voluntary "stepping across," a moment that is necessarily more than the usual continuance of meaning and intelligence.

Liminal situations and unanswerable questions elicit laughter or tears.[46] The intellect loses control. In weeping—in the gloom of melancholy emotion—the muscles relax; in laughter, they contract. Arendt allows the shock to make her taut rather than slack. There is no time to lose. At stake, after all, is the "deeper urge to get to the truth of things."

Yet laughter also carries us away. With all the ideas and images of monstrous murderers in our heads, of yelling SS men and their barking dogs so familiar from movies like *Schindler's List*, how else but in laughter would we be able to approach the *Schreibtischtäter* Eichmann, this bureaucratic perpetrator who simply stated as though it were the most unremarkable thing in the world that it didn't matter to him where they were deporting the Jews to because it wasn't his decision. She called him a buffoon. A comedian? She wanted to comprehend the world as it actually presented itself instead of limiting herself to what could be understood, in the sense of "deduced," from preconceived ideas, existing worldviews, or all the precious small and large lies we cling to.

In attempting to get closer to the truth, to let reality unsettle her own thoughts and conceptualizations, the woman who had hitherto spoken of the radicality of evil in a Kantian sense, now, in the final sentence of her book, launched the "banality of evil" into the world, an insight that owed its existence to, among other things, laughter, and under normal, rational circumstances would not have made it into the text as it did without being deduced and grounded in rationality.

Perhaps it is indeed the case, as Walter Benjamin assumes in "Central Park," his essay on Baudelaire, that in the act of laughing, one gains access to a region of one's self not otherwise accessible to reflection. The concept of the "banality of evil," unexpectedly launched into the world in the last paragraph of the book without being thought through, became the book's subtitle. Arendt wrote to Gershom Scholem that she had unlearned her conception of evil.

> It is indeed my opinion now that evil is never "radical," that it is only extreme, and that it possesses neither depth nor any demonic dimension. It can overgrow and lay waste the whole world precisely because it spreads like a fungus on the surface. [It is "thought-defying" as I said, because thought tries to reach some depth, to go to the roots, and the moment it concerns itself with evil, it is frustrated because there is nothing, That is its "banality."] Only the good has depth and can be radical. {If you read what Kant has to say about radical evil, you'll see that he doesn't mean much more than vulgar depravity, and that is a psychological, not a metaphysical concept.}[47]

This pathetic little Eichmann character and all his great, horrific deeds!

In order to get to the bottom of things, irony speaks about something that tragedy is incapable of addressing, because the enormity of emotion and suffering would have struck it dumb and the intellect would have gone limp. Arendt's laughter had loosened a moral fabric that theologians, philosophers, and scholars had woven all too tightly. They were unprepared for the phenomenon of motiveless mass murder and had nothing to say about it. Laughter had been recognized as an intellectual event.

Not long after the Eichmann book appeared, Arendt encountered a similar laughter in a less fraught context. She met Nathalie Sarraute, the French author of Russian extraction, at a dinner party and immediately sensed in her a kindred spirit. Sarraute's novels depict with eerie precision how utterly normal the co-optation of intellectuals is in the age of mass democracy, how they continue to speak without admitting to themselves that they have basically lost their bearings. "*La trahison des clercs*? Don't make me laugh. What have these creatures got that they could betray to begin with?" as Arendt quotes Sarraute.[48] Her novel *Le Planétarium* was a genuine comedy that "like all good comedy [is] concerned with something deadly serious," namely, with the fact that Sarraute uses her laughter to hold open a little door of hope through which she might one day advance toward "some tiny, undiluted, undistorted factual matter."[49]

THE DEED WITHOUT IMAGE

Born like Hannah Arendt in 1906, Adolf Eichmann seemed to her the prototype of a human being dependent on a leader and motivated by hackneyed phrases, norms, and platitudes. According to his own testimony, he had never tried to imagine the results of his actions. This is what Arendt terms "superficial." It is reminiscent of Nietzsche's description of the (last) human in the prologue to *Thus Spake Zarathustra*, at risk of more and more obstinately

adapting himself to mere superficial, outward aspects of his previous nature and allowing these flattened surfaces to define the
space of his sojourn on earth.

In the 1957 interview with the Dutch Nazi and journalist
Willem Sassen in Argentina, Eichmann described himself and
explained his membership in the National Socialist party: "This
cautious bureaucrat [i.e., himself] was at the same time a fanatical fighter for the freedom of the blood from which I come." But
when forced to depart from such clichés, when asked if after his
visit to Auschwitz he hadn't begun to think about what would
become of the people in the boxcars, he said, "My only foothold
was that I didn't know if any of them would die or go on living."[50]
He simply did not want to think about or try to imagine it.

Eichmann had lent a whole new dimension to this phenomenon, but it was not wholly novel to Arendt. In the *Duino Elegies*,
his late cycle of poems from 1923, Rainer Maria Rilke conjured up
the impending loss of world created by modernism:

> *Mehr als je*
> *fallen die Dinge dahin, die erlebbaren, denn,*
> *was sie verdrängend ersetzt, ist ein Tun ohne Bild.*

> More than ever
> things fall away, parts of experience, for
> what replaces, crowds them out, is acting without an image.

In order to describe Eichmann's "acting without an image,"
Arendt chose to analyze his comically macabre final words before
being executed. "He began by stating emphatically that he was a
Gottgläubiger [believer in God], to express in common Nazi fashion
that he was no Christian and did not believe in life after death.
He then proceeded: 'After a short while, gentlemen, *we shall all*

meet again. Such is the fate of all men....' In the face of death, he had found the cliché used in funeral oratory. Under the gallows, his memory played him the last trick; he was 'elated' and he forgot that this was his own funeral."[51]

Other catchwords and -phrases of Eichmann's generation lie buried in his utterances. "A little while, and ye shall not see me: and again, a little while, and ye shall see me, because I go to the Father" (John 16:16). These are words Jesus spoke to his disciples shortly before his death. And lines from a popular hit of the time

> *Warte, warte nur ein Weilchen,*
> *bald kommt auch das Glück zu dir.*
> *Mit dem ersten blauen Veilchen,*
> *klopft es leis' an deine Tür.*

> Wait, wait just a little while,
> soon happiness will also come to you.
> With the first blue violet,
> it will knock softly at your door.

were parodied in the film *M* (1931), in which Peter Lorre plays a child murderer:

> *Warte, warte nur ein Weilchen,*
> *dann kommt Haarmann auch zu Dir.*
> *Mit dem kleinen Hackebeilchen*
> *macht er Leberwurst aus dir.*

> Wait, wait just a little while,
> soon Haarmann [a contemporary German serial killer]
>   will also come to you.
> With his tiny little cleaver
> he'll make liverwurst out of you.

These two quotes, having degenerated into empty phrases, echo in Eichmann's "*in einem kurzen Weilchen*" (after a short little while). The cliché idyll evoked in a hit tune is unconsciously amalgamated with the biblical promise of life after death. Such an automatic association of empty words and phrases is undeniably ludicrous.

———

For Hannah Arendt, writing the Eichmann report was a liberating experience, as she later told her friend Mary McCarthy. In "The Hue and Cry," her discussion of *Eichmann in Jerusalem* for the *Partisan Review*, McCarthy had written that Arendt's book seemed to her "morally exhilarating." It was "not a hate-paean to totalitarianism but a paean of transcendence, heavenly music, like that of the final chorus of *Figaro* or the *Messiah*....The reader 'rose above' the terrible material of the trial or was borne aloft to survey it with his intelligence."[52] When the attacks on Arendt began, McCarthy apologized to her friend because she feared that these words could be misunderstood and used against her. But Arendt was pleased by the comparison with Handel, since she had in fact written the Eichmann book "in a curious state of euphoria." She didn't dare admit it, of course, or it would be seen as "proof positive that I have no 'soul,'" but in fact, ever since the book appeared she had felt "light-hearted" for the first time since the war.[53]

The path to this lightheartedness had been a long and difficult one: attending the trial, reading the documentation and the transcripts of the interrogations, meeting with survivors of the death camps and reading their testimonies, making her own observations, debating with friends and strangers, analyzing newspaper articles—all while constantly confronted by the incomprehensible reality of the will to destroy. The euphoria of which she wrote to Mary McCarthy may in fact have had its roots in the special happiness we feel when we have finally found the right metaphor for something that has been nagging us for a long time, a realization that at last casts light on what has remained in mental darkness. Arendt's laughter disturbed the world and its objects beyond sense and intellect for the instant of sudden inspiration she needed to discover the banality of evil. Of course, others had already formulated similar things, but Arendt had now exposed this concept to the world as something to be reckoned with. From then on, it was linked inextricably to her name.

LAUGHTER HAS CONSEQUENCES

In a 1945 essay, Arendt had called attention to the respectable appearance of Heinrich Himmler, who was "neither a Bohemian like Goebbels, nor a sex criminal like Streicher, nor a perverted fanatic like Hitler, nor an adventurer like Goering. He is a 'bourgeois' with all the outer aspect of respectability." Himmler had built up his terror organization "on the assumption that most people are…first and foremost jobholders, and good family men. It was Péguy, I believe, who called the family man the 'grand aventurier du 20e siècle'…an involuntary adventurer, who…for the sake of his pension, his life insurance, the security of his wife and children,…was ready to sacrifice his beliefs, his honor, and his human dignity."[54] Arendt's essay was a thought experiment, an attempt to approach such a figure intellectually. But she was still deeply uneasy about one question: Could it be that there were people who had never had any convictions, honor, or human dignity in the first place? By putting into words the idea of the "banality of evil" in the last sentence of her book, she had caught for herself and passed on to us a glimpse of the land of "How It Could Have Happened." It unleashed a storm. Simultaneously, and to a great extent because of that storm, a whole new chapter in her work began. First came two essays in 1964, "Personal Responsibility Under Dictatorship" and "Some Questions of Moral Philosophy." In the manuscript of her lecture "Some Questions of Moral Philosophy," she noted in 1965 that "the greatest evil perpetrated is the evil committed by nobodies, that is, by human beings who refuse to be persons."[55] Thus began work on *The Life of the Mind*; thinking about "thoughtlessness" led to thinking about what it means to think in the first place.

Making it clear that her later work grew out of the Eichmann debate, Arendt wrote, "In my report of it I spoke of 'the banality of evil.' Behind that phrase, I held no thesis or doctrine, although I was dimly aware of the fact that it went counter to our tradition of thought—literary, theological, or philosophic—about the phenomenon of evil."[56] Arendt knew that one cannot constantly rethink and question everything.

> Clichés, stock phrases, adherence to conventional, standardized codes of expression and conduct have the socially recognized function of protecting us against reality, that is, against the claim on our thinking attention that all events and facts make by virtue of their existence. If we were responsive to this claim all the time, we would soon be exhausted; Eichmann differed from the rest of us only in that he clearly knew of no such claim at all.
>
> It was this absence of thinking—which is so ordinary an experience in our everyday life, where we have hardly the time, let alone the inclination, to stop and think—that awakened my interest.[57]

Once she had made the idea of the banality of evil her own, she thought she could not evade the question of her right to use it. She asked herself if evil action without a motive was possible. And whether it was correct to assume that thought itself was "among the conditions that make men abstain from evil-doing or even actually 'condition' them against it?"[58] A laugh can have many consequences.

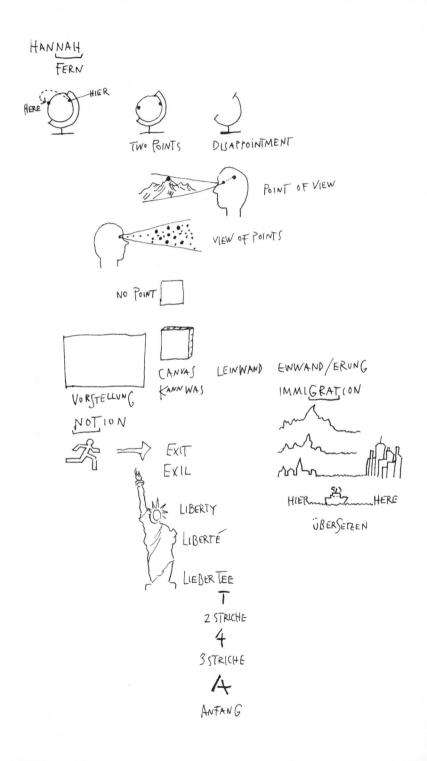

HANNAH
FERN

HERE / HIER

TWO POINTS

DISAPPOINTMENT

POINT OF VIEW

VIEW OF POINTS

NO POINT

CANVAS
KANN WAS

VORSTELLUNG
NOTION

LEINWAND

EINWAND/ERUNG
IMMIGRATION

EXIT
EXIL

LIBERTY
LIBERTÉ
LIEBER TEE

HIER — HERE
ÜBERSETZEN

T
2 STRICHE

4
3 STRICHE

A
ANFANG

TRANSLATION:
THE "ODDLY CIRCUITOUS PATH"

This then is everything and not enough
Yet lets you know perhaps that I'm still here.
I'm like the man who brought along a brick
To show the world the way his house had looked.
—Bertolt Brecht, "Motto"

Writing from Paris (and in French) in 1935, Hannah Arendt drew an interesting parallel in a text in honor of Martin Buber.[1] One hundred and fifty years previously, at the beginning of the emancipation of European Jews, Moses Mendelssohn's new translation of the Bible into German had led the way for young Jews to emerge from the ghetto, and in the 1920s, Martin Buber and Franz Rosenzweig's new translation of the Bible showed assimilated Jews the path back to the Jewish past. Both events happened through the "oddly circuitous path" of translation.[2] Moses Mendelssohn had arrived in Berlin in 1743 at the age of fourteen, entering the city through the gate reserved for Jews and livestock and knowing only West Yiddish and Hebrew. Much later, he decided to produce a new German translation of the Torah but to have it printed using Hebrew script rather than the Roman alphabet. According to Arendt, Mendelssohn's new translation allowed the Jews of his time, the majority of whom spoke Yiddish and could read only

Hebrew letters, entry into German and European culture. Buber and Rosenzweig's Bible translation was an achievement of parallel importance in the twentieth century, one which liberated the sacred text from both Christianizing and modern philosophical influences and created a German translation in which its Hebrew origins were again discernible. Via the "oddly circuitous path" of translation, she wrote, Buber and Rosenzweig had led the assimilated Jews back to Jewish culture. Arendt had fled Berlin for France in 1933, and her hymn of praise for Martin Buber, with its mention of Moses Mendelssohn, is based on the idea that in times of upheaval, translations have the ability to break down ghetto walls and punch through intellectual and cultural dead ends to open new avenues for thought. Like Mendelssohn, Buber and Rosenzweig had performed more than a simple act of linguistic transport. Through their translations, they had provided a new home for an alien spirit—one from a distant time and different cultural sphere. When the here and now into which this act of cultural transport occurs is open to dialogue, such a transfer has the power to impart new impulses to the receiving culture and to open up new images and spaces for thought. It was such an opening that Lambert Schneider, who was raised Catholic, had in mind when he persuaded Martin Buber to begin a German translation of the Torah in 1925 for his newly founded publishing house.[3]

Hannah Arendt grew up in the milieu of an educated German-Jewish family. She learned Latin and French and later Greek as well. In exile from the Nazis, she added English. She was never really able to speak Hebrew.

As late as 1927, she still described herself as "hopelessly assimilated," but in the face of the alarming increase of anti-Semitism in Germany, she became a critic of assimilation. Her declaration in 1933 that she would "never again get involved in any kind of intellectual business" expressed her shock. She had discovered that ordinary people had more civil courage and good common sense than her intellectual friends who had joined the National Socialists. As she later described the irrevocable break with tradition experienced by her entire generation and her own spiritual crisis, the rise of totalitarianism had "brought to light the ruin of our categories of thought and standards of judgment."[4] The world could no longer be comprehended through existing and traditional ideas about itself and mankind.[5] Could it be that the entirety of European humanism was irrelevant?

The émigré Arendt was to become the messenger of a double disaster: the bankruptcy of emancipation and assimilation on the one hand and the capitulation of thought and the ability to think on the other. Bearing this news, she fled first to France in 1933 and then to the United States in 1940. Unlike France, however, America then held no attraction for intellectuals from the Weimar Republic. How could one carry across the ocean the message that one had suffered in the flesh, deliver it to a land whose thinking had not been shaken by the experience of the First World War and that knew next to nothing about the radical and radicalized theoretical and aesthetic issues of modernity, next to nothing about the rise of fascism and Stalinism? How could an émigré keep people from "cart[ing] him up and down the country to exhibit him as the 'last European'"—Walter Benjamin's nightmare?[6]

It appeared easier for exiled composers and visual artists to find a foothold in America. Some became the precursors of the first wave of home-grown American modernism. The German émigré painter Hans Hofmann as well as Max Ernst and the surrealists with their experiments in automatism were the mentors and teachers of many of the abstract expressionists and colorfield painters. Robert Motherwell, Helen Frankenthaler, and Arshile Gorky were among Hofmann's students. In music, Arnold Schoenberg, who had broken open the traditions of listening during the Weimar era, passed on to John Cage and others the idea of bold aesthetic experiments that drew on nothing but the self. But it was another matter for writers and poets who had been driven from their linguistic environment and had only limited opportunities to develop in exile.

Hannah Arendt was thirty-four years old and obviously possessed of desperate courage when she landed in America. The terrible message she carried across the Atlantic was that the Europe of the Enlightenment, Reason, and the Rights of Man had been shattered and its tradition had collapsed. To move herself and others in this foreign land to reflect on this message, she would have to become "involved in intellectual business" again. So she wrote articles and began her great historical work *The Origins of Totalitarianism*, in which she attempted to translate for herself the message into thought. It appeared in English in 1949.

————

Among the challenges émigrés face is the step-by-step entry into the language, culture, and politics of their new country; it is an acculturation not to be confused with assimilation. Like Moses Mendessohn, Martin Buber, and Franz Rosenzweig, Arendt lived and acted in a multilingual and multicultural environment. She did not live between cultures nor did she build her house in the middle of the Atlantic. She had no desire to live in such an in-between realm, as she told Joachim Fest. "In the way I think and form judgments, I'm still from Königsberg. Sometimes I hide that from myself, but it's true. I'm an American only in my political heart, but there, completely."[7] To be from Königsberg meant, in this context, to be shaped by German, Jewish, and classical Greek culture—and also a bit by the Socialist ideals of her mother. In her essay "Creating a Cultural Atmosphere," published in *Commentary* in 1947, Arendt promotes the creation of a "culture for Jews."[8] It is evidence that after she arrived in America, she continued to think about the idea she had expressed in her 1935 essay on Buber: the far-reaching cultural significance of translation. According to her analysis, the Jews needed to withdraw—withdraw from modernity to the extent that it meant assimilation, withdraw from tradition to the extent that it concentrated on obeying religious laws or degenerated into mere folklore. Influenced by and elaborating on Walter Benjamin's secular interpretation of religious traditions, Arendt, at the time working for the publisher Schocken Books, demanded that the great metaphysical and postbiblical Jewish tradition be wrested from the theologians and carried over, or "trans-lated," into the secular life of modernity. Her own translation practice originated in the dilemma of her physical and intellectual isolation, which led to many things from then on having at least two denotations in her head. For her, as for Mendelssohn, Buber, and Rosenzweig, translation had, in addition to its linguistic dimension, an intellectual one—a dimension of emergence into something new that runs through her work, the dynamics of her thought, her writing, and her public voice in America and in Germany.

FIRST THREADS IN THE FABRIC OF PUBLIC DISCOURSE IN THE NEW COUNTRY

Der Aufbau (literally, "building up"), the first periodical in which Arendt published her work after her fortunate escape to America, was a rarity; the newspaper was bilingual and, in contrast to most newspapers for émigrés, had no particular political bias. For many German and Austrian exiles, *Aufbau* was a linguistic transit zone. German-language authors wrote in German and the small number of English-language authors wrote in English. Thus the paper offered the émigrés who had not yet adequately mastered the language of their host country an opportunity to weave some initial threads of their own into the fabric of public discourse, a place to catch their breath while continuing to put their thoughts into writing. One of the first quotations from the new language that Arendt wove into a German article for *Aufbau* was this excerpt from "Where Are the War Poets" by the Anglo-Irish poet Cecil Day-Lewis, born only a few years before Arendt:

It is the logic of our time,
No subject for immortal verse,
That we, who lived by honest dreams,
defend the bad against the worst.

They are a foreign-language inlay in a German-language essay on Jewish politics, one small bridge along her path of trans-lation. Implicitly, the poet says, "We exiles know we are not alone. We share our concerns, our 'honest dreams.' You can see that the world has become a question for all men."

With the loss of their language and their native cultural context, everything natural, simple, and unforced has been lost as well. This is an unalterable fact. Exile means the certainty that from now on, every expression and encounter, every feeling, gesture, and reaction must be "carried over," translated (from the Latin *translatum*, "carried across"), that is, emphasized, explained, and transported. From now on, the difference in linguistic expression alone will always be an obstacle, or rather, a threshold the émigré must cross at every moment, in every word and gesture. As Gershom Scholem said, "Nothing is...in the right place. Everything is in exile."

A FESTIVAL OF CONTAMINATION

In the early 1940s, Arendt, who all her life never stopped being "a little worried...about the language problem,"[9] needed the help of an intermediary for all her texts that could not be published by *Aufbau*. For her texts to cross the threshold and reach the public discourse of her new country, someone had to correct her English. Her friends Randall Jarrell and Rose Feitelson were the first to transport her texts across the linguistic border by correcting her *Denglisch*. It was a painful experience not to be able to express what she had to say.

But Arendt recognized the limitation as an opportunity. Translation, which at the beginning of her residence in America was a necessity springing from the problem of being in exile from her native linguistic environment, became in the course of time a vital spur to thought. As late as 1964, twenty-three years after her arrival, she confessed to Günter Gaus:

> I write in English but I have never lost my distance to it. There
> is an enormous distance between one's mother tongue and all

other languages. For me it's terribly easy to express: in German I know a fairly large number of German poems by heart. They're always moving around somewhere "in the back of my mind." I allow myself to say things in German that I would never say in English.... You can forget your mother tongue.... I have seen it happen. These people speak the foreign language better than I do.... But it's a language of one cliché after another, because the productivity one has in one's own language is cut off when one forgets it.[10]

Like Arendt, other émigrés warned of the danger of falling into what Jean Améry called a "loathsome émigré mish-mash."[11] But unlike many other German and Austrian exile writers, Hannah Arendt used her native language not just at her desk, in intellectual dialogue with herself and with German-language authors both living and dead. She also spoke German with her husband, the poet and philosopher Heinrich Blücher, and with the friends in her peer group, all of whom "carried across" like her: the Yiddish poet Chanan Klenbort who, published under the nom de plume Ayalti, emigrated from Russia and gave her Hebrew lessons in Paris; the painter Carl Heidenreich, a friend of Blücher's she had also come to know in Paris; Peter Huber, a veteran of the Spanish Civil War; and the author Charlotte Beradt. Later, her circle of German-speaking friends came to include Hermann Broch, Hilde Fränkel, and Julie Braun-Vogelstein.

To remain alive, language must constantly engage with the present. It needs the renewing power of poetry and the dynamic and sometimes even offensive impulses of metaphor (Greek *metapherein*, "to transfer, carry across"). Metaphors, associations, and concepts such as autonomy, the rights of man, and freedom carry thought out of pure perception of concrete things and offer insights into the construction of language which, despite everything, holds the human world together.[12] Thus art is a constant give-and-take: by exploiting the visible to designate the invisible,[13] metaphor inspires the writer to launch new images into the world. For a foreigner, active participation in this productive give-and-take in the new language must remain long out of reach.

The Nobel laureate Herta Müller, a border-crossing exile from both the Romanian dictatorship and the linguistic environment of her own regional dialect of German, gives us an idea of the truth inherent in this give-and-take of images:

> I don't trust language. I know best in my own case that in order to be precise, language always takes something that doesn't belong to it. I don't know why images are so larcenous. Why does the most valid comparison steal characteristics it has no right to? Only by means of invention does the unexpected happen, and it proves to be the case again and again that only in the invented surprise within the sentence do we begin to approach reality.[14]

It takes a long time for any exiled writer to recognize such "invented surprises" in texts in her new language.

Hannah Arendt grew up with German poetry in her ears and could never get anything out of dadaism, the artistic and literary movement that translated the terrors of reality into a material dismemberment of words and letters. She was not a poet herself and it obviously never occurred to her to be creatively inventive with the material of the new language like her friend Robert Gilbert, a popular songwriter who rhymed *shtetl* with *Popocatépetl*, or bicultural writers of today like the Japanese-German Yoko Tawada in *Sprachpolizei* (Language police) or the Turkish-German Emine Sevgi Özdamar in *Mutterzunge* (Mother tongue). Arendt made no attempt to overcome the obstacles of the new language by dreaming up bilingual associations.

One of the first steps taken by Arendt and Heinrich Blücher to reconnoiter the territory of the English language was to organize poetry evenings with their friend Randall Jarrell, the poet and sometime book review editor for the *Nation* who also corrected the English in some of her early postwar texts. Jarrell would read English poems to her, as she related in her eulogy for him, "old and new, only rarely his own.... He opened up for me a whole new world of sound and meter, and he taught me the specific gravity of English words, whose relative weight, as in all languages, is ultimately determined by poetic usage and standards."[15]

———

Of course, Arendt also read American political theory, but she knew that the genius of a language is nourished mainly by its use in literature. In their nakedness and directness, the words of poets break open analytic language and grant the freedom and encouragement to create one's own language and meaning. Poetic metaphor is itself a translation and a celebration of contamination.

This leads to another insight: it is the poets, she noted in her essay on Hermann Broch, who wrestle desperately with the break in tradition. They are bound together by their concern to reconquer the lost territory of commonality. In translation and in the sensual quality of metaphor—in other words, in what Aristotle called "giving metaphorical life to lifeless things"—the (totalitarian) danger of decoupling thought from reality and experience is reversed. According to Arendt's essay on Benjamin, the only people who still believe in the world are the poets; they cannot afford to be alienated from it.

In the linguistic exile of a foreign language, the metaphors, images, myths, rhythms, and rhymes that are part of everyone's (and especially the poets') flesh and blood since childhood lose their associative power. For a long time, the new arrival is excluded from idiosyncratic participation in the illuminating and world-creating power of metaphor in the new language.

THE GIRL FROM ABROAD

Arendt did not believe in collective identity. She was well aware of the fragility of her existence in the postwar world: a Jewish woman married to a gentile and writing about Jewish affairs as if oblivious of the culture of remembrance and the basic concepts of Jewish historiography. In a letter to Martin Heidegger in 1950, Arendt wrote that she had never felt like a German woman and had long since ceased to feel like a Jewish woman. "I feel just like what I am now, after all, the girl from abroad."[16] Schiller's image of the girl from abroad who gives the gift of fruit ripened "in a different light" and in "a more fortunate nature" limns the risky undertaking of an intellectual existence but also the courage and grace with which Arendt settled in America.[17]

Language articulates thought. The world is given to each of us at birth in a particular language and only gradually can thought move beyond its boundaries. From 1946 to 1948, Hannah Arendt worked as an editor at the quadrilingual (English, German, Hebrew, and Yiddish) publisher Shocken Books. She imagined it as an ideal meetingplace for foreigners and Americans, and planned a small volume on the topic of translation, with essays by Franz Rosenzweig, Walter Benjamin, and Hermann Broch.[18] All three essays oppose in very different ways the assimilationist ideal of turning foreign-language originals into works that sound like they were written in the target language.

It was a lecture given by her friend Hermann Broch that had inspired her to put together the collection. At the end of his highly poetic analysis of the untranslatability of Matthias Claudius's poem "Der Mond ist aufgegangen" (The Moon Has Risen), Broch proposed the thesis that in every work of German literature there was an echo of the world of German poetry and fairy tales—fog, forest, moon, dragons, elves—and this echo must reverberate in all translations.

The Bible translator Franz Rosenzweig had already made a similar argument in 1924, but in less poetic language. In his well-known criticism that "foreign texts get translated into already existing German," we hear an anticipation of Hannah Arendt's attack on the linguistic clichés of the refugees. Rosenzweig formulated his demand for an echo of the original culture in the translation: "The translator makes himself into the mouthpiece for another's voice, which he makes audible across the abyss of space and time. If the foreign voice has something to say, then the language into which he translates it must afterward look different than it did before.... For with the foreign voice comes also the entire spirit of the foreign language."[19]

In Benjamin's essay on translation as well, what is worth translating is located precisely in what resists exact translation, thereby complementing and expanding the target language. Separating the work from its customary context is a first step toward "liberating" it—that is, freeing it for some new perspective. According to Benjamin, this "ever-renewed...flowering" of the original through the act of translation transforms it into something new that, in the context of the target language, reveals itself as a "wind" from the source language.[20] Translations keep language in a dynamic of development.

Writing in a foreign language confronted Arendt with a dilemma. Her style, full of explicit and implicit quotations and images through which other voices and views invade and interrupt her own observations, caused difficulties when it came to transporting her thoughts into a new linguistic realm.[21] She thought in images and verses that she had "in the back of her mind," as she expressed it. But how could she quote, how could she set up a polyphony of voices in a foreign language when there were no—or at least, no usable—English translations of the voices that echoed in her head while she wrote, voices she wanted to be heard through her writing?

She was involved as a native-speaker consultant in the translation of Kafka's diaries from 1946 to 1948. Later she advised the American translators of Heidegger, Jaspers, and Rilke. And she taught Plato, Kant, Machiavelli, and Spinoza in the deconstructivist readings of German modernism. The girl from abroad, the former student of Heidegger, brought to the United States her knowledge of interwar European humanistic modernism and its collapse. One focus of her discussions with American writers and translators was conceptual consistency. For instance, in a letter to Glenn Gray, a translator of Heidegger, she advises that

> the German "Vorstellung" is generally best translated with "notion," not with "idea." The word "idea" should really be left

for "Idee." Under no circumstances, I think, can you say "notion" for "Begriff." To have translated "Begriff" by "notion" is among the most grievous mistranslations of Hegel. "Begriff" should really be always "concept" or "conception."[22]

What can one do in the face of the fact that "concept" in English does not have the same consistency as *Begriff* in German and that metaphors convey different contexts? How can one make do when a line of poetry translated from one's own language evokes no associations—or different associations—in the target language? It is a well-known and frequently encountered phenomenon that translations of poems often have quite different meanings in the context of the target language than in the original.

Arendt had to keep all of these aspects in mind while writing. The technique of textual cross-fading, or choosing images and quotations that would resonate in the ears of both the native and the foreign reader, was not part of Arendt's style. Instead, she placed side by side in montage "Willst Du Dein Herz mir schenken, so fang es heimlich an"[23] and William Blake's "Never seek to tell thy love, love that never told can be."

In the difficult process of translating concepts from one language into another, detailed knowledge of the respective cultural idiosyncrasies is required. After reading Arendt's collection of portraits titled *Men in Dark Times*, Mary McCarthy noted that she liked best the portraits Arendt had written originally in English. For her, those figures, including Walter Benjamin, were particularly vivid. But it was different with the texts that had been translated from German into English.

There are wonderful thoughts in the Lessing speech but sometimes they have to be sensed, rather than clearly perceived,
through a fog of approximative translation, e.g., "humanity,"
"humaneness," "humanitarianism," which are occasionally
treated as synonymous and occasionally not. Your habit of making linguistic distinctions is not well served by your translators,
whose language, far from achieving precision, creates a blur...
a key term ought to be pinned down for the reader. Maybe by
expansion, the best way in English, which is so impoverished in
its philosophical vocabulary. When you write yourself in English, you're conscious of the problem and find a means of making
your distinctions visible and palpable, but your translators often
don't bother.[24]

Even in the pieces she wrote in English, Arendt kept alive the
spirit of German language, philosophy, and poetry. She discovered that it was "incomparably easier to make a philosophical
statement in German than in English," but that English and to
a certain extent French were much better for political thought.[25]
According to Arendt, language and thought cannot be separated.
As she told Robert Lowell, her own thinking and writing combined "English instantness" with "German philosophical discipline."[26] After reading *The Origins of Totalitarianism*, Scholem
wrote from faraway Israel, "A book that undertakes to think in
fundamental categories must be a rare bird in the USA, given the
prevailing wishy-washy state of all concepts." And he wondered if
she hadn't caused a good deal of astonishment in New York.[27]

In fact, her "German philosophical discipline" often alienated people. It is not surprising that for many years, Arendt's English was much less vivid than her German: "born and educated

in Germany as, no doubt, you can hear." Thus begins her thank-you speech for the Sonning Prize in 1975, the last year of her life. When a critic wrote that her English is full of "incoherent sentences and semantic errors" and also criticized Arendt's use of a triad of concepts unusual in English—"labor," "work," and "action"—in *The Human Condition*, he overlooked the fact that the positing of her own concepts and metaphors is exactly what lends specific weight to what is new in her thinking.[28] Her choice of nonstandard terms gives her fresh ideas the élan necessary to have a powerful impact on her readers. In choosing "labor," Arendt evokes the organizations of the working class in such phrases as "labor power" and "labor movement," since in her imagination, "work"—the actual Marxist equivalent for German *Arbeit*—was presumably too connected with the product of labor.

———

Like Schiller's girl, Arendt arrived in America bearing fruits from abroad, "ripened" first by the light of European intellectual history, but then also by its collapse. She rubbed people in America the wrong way—not least during the McCarthy era when, as Arendt wrote to Jaspers, teaching European authors (including of course the ancient Greeks) was frowned upon. Her habit of thinking through every question remained foreign to her English-speaking audience, yet precisely this "thinking through" would be one of her greatest gifts to the American intelligentsia.[29]

American artists responded to her. They recognized Arendt as a new voice in their intellectual and spiritual environment. She thought with all her senses and with conceptual stringency. As Randall Jarrell wrote to her, "The reader feels and understands at the same time."[30] Arendt's *The Human Condition* of 1958 was a fundamentally new conception of what we are doing when we act. The triadic structure of the work is grounded in the Greek tradition. W. H. Auden remarked, "It would not be inaccurate…to call *The Human Condition* an essay in Etymology, a re-examination of what we think we mean, what we actually mean and what we ought to mean when we use such words as nature, world, labor, work, action, private, public, social, political etc."[31] He praised the work for its diagnostic courage to air out traditional concepts, not to dismiss them but to rethink their place in the present.

Arendt's examination of basic concepts also spoke to the art critic Harold Rosenberg. He titled his *New York Times* review of *Between Past and Future* "Concepts We Live By."

We live our lives with the help of the concepts we form of the world. They enable an author to make the transition from shock to observation to finally creating space for action—for writing and speaking. Just as laws guarantee a public space for political action, conceptual thought ensures the existence of the four walls within which judgment operates. Walter Benjamin pointed out this necessary conceptual basis and the resulting direct connection between thinking and literature when he described prose that "lacks any theoretical foundation" as a "stammering" of forgotten marionette-like shapes.[32] Along with her work on a conceptual foundation, spinning the thread of Ariadne in the labyrinth of the present, Arendt made use of a special quality of English literature that she found congenial—its ability to breathe new life into extremely prosaic words and idiomatic expressions.

A MULTIPLE METAMORPHOSIS

The commonly accepted idea of an "original text" does not apply to Arendt's writings. Her "original texts"—that is, the English versions of her major works—are always already translations. There is no such thing as a single "vision" composed in the original language from which all others versions deviate.[33] Instead, the English and German versions of her main works always represent two "originals" that differ somewhat from each other despite being closely related. Some chapters of *The Origins of Totalitarianism* were composed first in English, others first in German, but Arendt found no significance difference between the two languages in this work.[34] All of her later major works were first composed entirely in English.

Vladimir Nabokov, who left the land of his native Russian as a young man and wrote the greater portion of his literary works in English, commented on the Russian edition of his autobiographical work:

> For the present, final, edition of *Speak, Memory* I have not only introduced basic changes and copious additions into the initial English text, but have availed myself of the corrections I made while turning it into Russian. This re-Englishing of a Russian reversion of what had been an English re-telling of Russian memories in the first place, proved to be a diabolical task, but some consolation was given me by the thought that such multiple metamorphosis, familiar to butterflies, had not been tried by any human before.[35]

Like Nabokov's work, Hannah Arendt's books went through their own metamorphosis. Thoughts that originated in the context of German and European intellectual history and the experience of their collapse, composed in American English and rooted in its associative style, are brought back into German.[36] A comparison of the two versions is revealing; in the German text,

Arendt deconstructs idiomatic expressions and makes explicit many quotes and references that must have already resonated "in the back of her mind" while she was writing in English. Moreover, the German text deploys powerful stylistic effects — repetition, alliteration, emphasis, rhythm. But bilinguality does not mean that one language is impoverished while the other is rich. Arendt's voice sounds different in each separate linguistic realm. In some passages, the original English version follows different images and trains of thought from the original German version. But how did these different visions arise? Arendt retained a lifelong distance from English, which from 1950 on was the primary language of her public voice. As she summed it up in 1975, if she had ever done anything consciously for European civilization, it consisted of an explicit resolve not to exchange her mother tongue for any other language, "no matter whether it was offered to me or forced upon me."[37]

It took three years for her magnum opus *The Human Condition* (1958) to appear in German under the title *Vita activa* (1961). The work of translation was tedious but productive. Charlotte Beradt, a journalist and friend, prepared a rough translation from the English. This intermediate step, probably undertaken as a result of time pressure and meant to be provisional, turned out to be serendipitous. Arendt had composed in English a thought that was perhaps originally conceived in German and it was then backtranslated by Beradt into its (actual) mother tongue. Thus the initial linguistic foreignness in which the actual thought had been written down could be provisionally preserved in German. Arendt now had at her disposal a rudimentary text that she could carry over through her own independent intellectual and linguistic gesture into German. Yet despite this successful intermediate step—the construction of a rough translation by someone else—translating her own works remained a "diabolical task" since, among other reasons, she had to check the German citations, correct errors, and add passages of explanation or clarification.[38] The German versions of the works she wrote originally in English were simultaneously revisions, which she then used for subsequent editions of the English works. The better her English became, the harder it was for her to translate her works into German. "Devil take this bilinguality!" she wrote to Jaspers in 1963.[39]

When writing in the one or the other language, Arendt sometimes had their respective reading publics in mind. In Freiburg in 1967, for instance, she gave a lecture on Walter Benjamin that was printed in the journal *Merkur*. Among other things, she depicted for the German audience the hostility confronting Jewish scholars in the Weimar Republic if they wanted to pursue a career in academia. (In the front row of the lecture hall that evening sat Martin Heidegger, who, as rector, had signed the racially motivated expulsion of Edmund Husserl from Freiburg University in 1933.) In the English version of the Benjamin essay, much less space and weight is devoted to this piece of German history.[40]

Conversely, in the English version of her essay on Bertolt Brecht, Arendt provided her American readership with a lengthy description of the ravages of the House Un-American Activities Committee and in addition criticized the decision of the U.S. military administration in Germany to deny Brecht a visa to Munich after he had flown from the United States to Switzerland in 1947. Brecht thereupon went to East Berlin instead. Arendt concludes, "This turned out to be almost equally unfortunate for Germany and for Brecht himself."[41] This sentence is not in the German version. In this essay, published originally in 1967 in the *New York Review of Books*, Arendt developed her own unique metaphor-rich English style and quoted Brecht's poems in German, with English translations. After reading it, Glenn Gray wrote her, "No one would think that you were not nurtured by English poetry."[42]

Arendt's works are still being translated into other languages from the original English versions. Yet we know today that the original German version of *Vita activa* serves as a prime example of an Arendt text that not only contains important annotations lacking in the English original but also has deeper intellectual and literary roots, as well as more far-reaching influence.

HOW LUCKY WE ARE THAT YOU HAVE COME.
Arendt's active bilingualism culminated in her 1963 book *On Revolution*. Just as the Bible instantiates the great Jewish heritage of Mendelssohn and Buber, the U.S. Constitution represents the great American heritage underlying *On Revolution*. Like the Torah and the Bible for prewar Germans, the Constitution for Americans, as Arendt well knew, was "part of their flesh and blood."[43] Arendt had studied the Constitution in 1951 while preparing to become a citizen. More than ten years later, at a time when the American republic was suffering a deep inner erosion, *On Revolution* reminded readers of the glorious past, the yearning for freedom, and the revolutionaries' ruminations on freedom's fragility. She seized a memory "as an image that flashes up at the instant it can be recognized," as Walter Benjamin put it in "Theses on the Philosophy of History."[44]

The results of her study were by no means positive. In *The Human Condition*, she warns that mass society threatens to replace the individual with *Homo faber*, and shortly before the end of *On Revolution*, she proclaims that the revolutionary spirit has "failed to find its appropriate institution.... There is nothing that could compensate for this failure or prevent it from becoming final, except memory and recollection."[45]

One might consider this a pessimistic view of the world—a "tragedy," as she wrote to Jaspers—yet it is one that also "warms and lightens the heart"[46] because despite the revolution's failure, through Arendt's evocation of its memory in writing, the power of revolutionary association to create community and promulgate laws gains immediacy in the eyes of her readers as something of simplicity and greatness. In fact, she kindles in the reader a revolutionary yearning. It is as if the historical personages are precipitated out of the objective historical account and returned to the living, internal stage of their own world, which in turn is conceived as a public space. The effect is grounded in Plato's idea that literature about tragic things is not, as Aristotle posited, written to make people experience empathy. Instead, its principal aim is to keep alive in the reader (who by reading rehearses taking action) the presence of values and concepts in a world where values have been lost, and to reinvigorate moribund collective ideas. This is the idea that shaped *The Human Condition* as well as Arendt's essay "Tradition and the Modern Age."[47]

In her retelling of American revolutionary history, Arendt breathed new life into the spirit of confederation and the idea of fresh beginnings. In 1963, Arendt, the German immigrant and sharp critic of the Russian Revolution's turn from its roots in democratic workers' and soldiers' councils to the totalitarian state, reclaimed for herself and her American readers the foundations of their political home. She *translated* for herself and the fellow citizens of her political homeland the rejuvenating power of their own revolutionary history. Only a foreigner, a pariah, could have done so. In the middle of the cold war, at the height of the Cuban missile crisis, an immigrant who had personally experienced the erosion of the Weimar Republic recognized the mighty power of America's foundational myths: the Founding Fathers and their ideal republic of deliberative councils as the center of political action. One can imagine that her book did not find a universally sympathetic hearing and was dismissed or misunderstood by some as a gesture of gratitude toward her adoptive country. Both her mixture of conservative and revolutionary ideas and her strict separation of the political and the social met with incomprehension. Arendt had written not a proper history of revolt but rather an admonitory book, an attempt to recover the lost treasure of revolution, especially the American Revolution. And *On Revolution* elicited a lively response from the student movement, the peace groups, and the neighborhood organizations that were being founded in mid-1960s America.

After this book, Arendt's voice in the United States grew even more powerful. She contributed influential essays to the discussions of the Vietnam War and the Watergate affair, addressing such topics as the contamination of the political sphere by boundless lies, the use of imagery as a tool for the indoctrination of the American public, and the transformation of an initially production-based society into a consumer-based one, bringing with it the domination of public relations experts and professional manipulators of opinion. With her pariahlike perspective and the experience of totalitarianism in the back of her mind (ever since her arrival she had been the messenger of ill tidings), Arendt diagnosed an imperiled politics in the democratic state.

Arendt may have recalled a passage Kafka crossed out in the manuscript of *The Castle* about the hopes that the village girl Olga places in the newly arrived K.:

> You have an amazing overview.... Sometimes you help me with a word. It must be because you come from abroad. But we with our sad experience and constant fear, we are frightened by the very creak of a board yet don't defend ourselves, and when one of us is frightened the next gets frightened too without even knowing why. It's no way to be able to judge things correctly.... How lucky we are that you have come.[48]

The very last essay she wrote was titled "Home to Roost," a reference to Malcolm X's speech after the assassination of John F. Kennedy, in which he said that all the chickens were coming home to roost and American imperialism was now reaping what it had sown. In her essay, an elaboration of a lecture she gave on the two-hundredth anniversary of the American Revolution, Arendt warned of the disintegration of democratic power, which could produce a historic break comparable to the one that had ushered in the destruction of the European polity by totalitarianism:

> We may very well stand at one of those decisive turning points of history which separate whole eras from each other. For contemporaries entangled, as we are, in the inexorable demands of daily life, the dividing lines between eras may be hardly visible when they are crossed; only after people stumble over them do the lines grow into walls which irretrievably shut off the past.[49]

The eulogy for the girl from abroad that appeared in the *New Yorker* shortly after her death declared, "Some days ago Hannah Arendt died, at the age of sixty-nine. We felt a tremor, as if some counterweight to all the world's unreason and corruption had been removed."[50] How lucky it was that she had come.

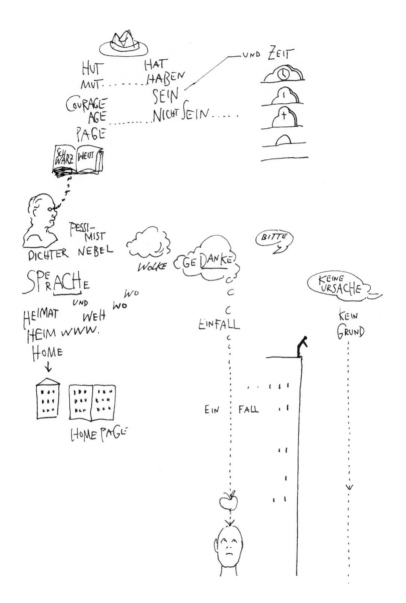

FORGIVENESS: THE DESPERATE SEARCH FOR A CONCEPT OF REALITY

You in the night, learning
to unlearn the world.
—Nelly Sachs

In September 1946, Hannah Arendt happened upon one of the last speeches of the Jewish labor leader Berl Katznelson, delivered at a conference of Socialist youth leaders in Palestine in 1944. "My Lord, you have to admire him," she wrote to Gershom Scholem. It was "the best thing about Fascism" she had ever seen in print.[1] What had impressed her so strongly? The fifty-seven-year-old Katznelson (1887–1944), a committed Socialist and early Zionist, had left tsarist Russia for Palestine in 1909 at the age of twenty-two. As a close associate of the future prime minister David Ben-Gurion, he went on to both set up the health insurance system and found the newspaper of the workers' movement. In his 1944 speech, he urged his listeners to allow themselves to "be confused" by the times. It was no longer possible to cling to traditional notions of nationalism, socialism, and fascism and seal themselves off from reality with images of the world inherited from the nineteenth century. They had all believed for too long in the unifying power of the nation and the disappearance of social classes under socialism. Now they must realize that their humane ideals, "the cultural distillation of generations," lay in ruins, defiled and desecrated. From the roots of Garibaldi had grown Mussolini and from the roots of the Russian Revolution, Stalin. How could they not be confused?

Until then, fascism had been seen as conservative or reactionary, but in reality, he continued, it had long since proved to be a revolutionary and destructive force, ready to make a pact with anyone in order to further its own plans for world domination. Fascism was no longer an outlaw movement, he argued. It had moved center stage with the goal of replacing the humane ideal with a system based on lies, cruelty, and humiliation.

Katznelson warned especially that in the struggle with their foes, they could become more and more like them, for even in Palestine there was a growing "admiration of fascism's *power*" as well as the idea that one could weigh humanitarian principles against each other. "Do we, the bitter enemies of fascism, not share in so greatly exaggerating the value of force and placing it at the very head of our scale of values?"[2]

The experiences of an entire generation—and not just in Palestine—were behind Katznelson's appeal to the youth leaders to allow themselves to be confused. Nationalism and socialism, the ideologies of the nineteenth century, no longer held up. The reversal of tradition and the revaluation of values as conceived by Marx, Kierkegaard, and Nietzsche were no help either, and even Heidegger's attempt to "approach tradition so closely with new concepts that it can still be understood" belonged to the past.[3] In Arendt's opinion, the paradoxical patterns of thought typical for the years of the Weimar Republic arose automatically when people like Rilke and Heidegger attempted to "comprehend modern experience with traditional concepts."[4] In the *Denktagebuch*, her "intellectual diary," Arendt notes that paradoxes were typical of intellectual thought following the First World War, when the break with tradition was already discernible but not yet completed, "to the extent that consciousness of the break still assumed the memory of tradition and made the break reparable in principle." So that even when thinking in paradoxes, one could lean on the "banister" of tradition.[5] "The rupture was completed only after the Second World War, when it was no longer even perceived as a rupture."[6] National Socialism signified the fall of all the restraints, limits, and rules of coexistence that had until then survived into the secularized world. It had cut all the residual ties between generations, devastated all areas of life, and rendered useless all instruments of understanding. Humanism, which had been thought to hold the world together, was in danger of proving simply irrelevant. Serious thought after the break with tradition had to allow itself to be reinitiated by precisely that deep and irreparable rupture.

———

Where certainty ceases, thinking begins; the knower sets off into uncertainty. Both traditional ideas and their inverse had to be abandoned as supports. As the life of Katznelson shows, to achieve such freedom there has to be first the ability to allow oneself to be confused by intrusive reality along with diagnostic and intellectual courage. How can our intellect accept what it sees and hears, how can it deal with what happens to us? How does one reach a new, adequate concept of the real? How can one unlearn the known and turn it into the unknown?

THE CAREER OF A CONCEPT

One of the central concepts Arendt herself unlearned—gave up and reconceived—during work on her political theory was the idea of forgiveness. In the *Denktagebuch* of 1950, forgiveness is still embedded in the Christian tradition of love of one's fellow man, and Arendt could conceive of it only as a gesture of superiority, a dead end. More than ten years later, in 1961, the human ability to forgive had become one of the pillars of her political theory. This is not the place to address the question of whether Arendt's concept of forgiveness gave rise to new approaches in the field of moral philosophy. Instead, I will discuss how she needed to reject the traditional understanding of forgiveness in order to overcome an intellectual affliction. Traditional forgiveness was no longer adequate for the present day. It had to be separated from its Christian context, deconstructed, and unlearned, i.e., learned anew. We shall follow the paths of thought by which she shaped a new presence for forgiveness.

THE POSTWAR DILEMMA

In 1949, the organization Jewish Cultural Reconstruction sent Hannah Arendt to Germany in order to salvage and return to the Jewish people surviving archives, manuscripts, libraries, and ceremonial objects stolen by the Nazis. The landscape through which she traveled was still her homeland, but the cities lay in ruins. Everywhere she went, she encountered people who were all eagerly preoccupied with the task of rebuilding: both anti-Fascists and longtime Nazis—librarians, museum directors, former perpetrators as well as mere hangers-on. In between there was the relief of reunions with her old friends Karl Jaspers and Ernst Grumach—like lodestars in stormy seas.[7] But how ought she to behave to the others with whom she had to negotiate in postwar Germany, the silent and the blind, obsessed with reconstruction and, at best, hoping to undo the unforgivable, and at worst, to simply ignore it? As she had written to Karl Jaspers in 1947, the genocide of the Jews could not be comprehended by any existing political categories or judged by any existing judicial instruments. That was precisely what made it monstrous: "The Germans are burdened now with thousands or tens of thousands or hundreds of thousands of people who cannot be adequately punished within the legal system; and we Jews are burdened with millions of innocents, by reason of which every Jew alive today can see himself as innocence personified."[8]

Personifications of innocence are saints who have no stake in community. Law was helpless in the face of the reality of the gas chambers. The deeds of the Nazis beggared the imagination. There was no way to mete out punishment for them. Moreover, justice failed in its second social task. Usually, perpetrators are punished and then returned to society. In our idea of justice, punishment and absolution go hand in hand, for both actions afford a chance to reconstitute the community that has been ruptured by the crime. But that was unimaginable with respect to the Nazi perpetrators.[9] Nevertheless, of course, they had to be tried and punished for their deeds. Later, in the last words of *Eichmann in Jerusalem*, Arendt would justify the death penalty for Eichmann in words she wishes the judges in Jerusalem had used in their sentence:

Just as you supported and carried out a policy of not wanting to share the earth with the Jewish people and the people of a number of other nations—as though you and your superiors had any right to determine who should and who should not inhabit the world—we find that no one, that is, no member of the human race, can be expected to want to share the earth with you. This is the reason, and the only reason, you must hang.[10]

Crimes that proved unpunishable and thus also unforgivable belonged, in Arendt's eyes, to what Immanuel Kant called "radical evil":

When the impossible was made possible it became the unpunishable, unforgivable absolute evil which could no longer be understood and explained by the evil motives of self-interest, greed, covetousness, resentment, lust for power, and cowardice; and which therefore anger could not revenge, love could not endure, friendship could not forgive.[11]

————

While Hannah Arendt recognized revenge as a possible action in her *Denktagebuch* of 1950, she found forgiveness out of brotherly love incomprehensible. She still could not envision a new understanding of forgiveness. It was for her an obtuse concept. But she did begin to develop an ethical yardstick for interpersonal relations. The question was "how seriously the individual takes being involved and impacted and does not avoid the issue by appealing to so-called world history or becoming 'noble.'"[12] That took care of the demands of the present. One had to allow one's comfortable certainties to be unsettled by the plethora of urgent realities. And yet, how could she reconnect thinking to her own experience?[13] How could language protect itself from being swamped by mere chatter as well as from losing itself in deductive reasoning, in order to again give mankind what Heinrich Blücher called "real nourishment"?

THE BLANK CANVAS

As the philosopher Gilles Deleuze put it, no painter ever stands before a completely blank canvas, no author ever sits before a blank page. In fact, the surface confronting the modern artist is full of inherited images that must first be cleared from the imagination before one can begin to create one's own. Deleuze describes this work as a "desperate struggle" that can take years or even decades.[14] Hannah Arendt went through just such a struggle to unlearn Christian forgiveness and relearn forgiveness as the foundation of politics. The *Denktagebuch* records the stations of her unlearning, the work of clearing away and reimagining.

According to the Grimm brothers' great historical dictionary of German, the act of *verzeihen* (to forgive, pardon, excuse) is first and foremost a matter between two people and means "to forgive an offense directed at one's person, an invasion or intrusion into one's own interests and not to punish it, that is, not to retaliate, but of one's own free will to overlook it; also: to not bear a grudge for the injustice one has suffered."[15] Forgiveness is an act of free will and cannot be required, a one-sided "discretionary" action aimed at absolving something that has happened between people from the consequences inherent in that deed. Etymologically, *verzeihen* developed from the verb *verzichten* (to forgo), forgoing a legal claim, for example, for the sake of another person. The verb *vergeben* (to forgive), by contrast, is associated with *geben* (to give), a disinterested, unconditional gift of love and thus of the Christian love for one's fellow man. In modern usage, *vergeben* and *verzeihen* are practically synonymous, although their different origins still echo in the two words (Arendt herself did not rigorously distinguish between them), and the Christian justification for forgiveness of one's fellow man still influences both popular and philosophical thinking about the concept.

This traditional idea of forgiveness also initially dominated Arendt's entries in the *Denktagebuch*. In *The Human Condition*, she rid herself of the idea that forgiveness and brotherly love were related concepts, because it seemed to her a dead end. There is hardly another concept in *The Human Condition*, her attempt to reestablish the foundations of the political, that has evoked such a huge and controversial reaction as her newly realized idea of forgiveness. How did this concept, "which — perhaps because of its religious context, perhaps because of the connection with love attending its discovery — has always been deemed unrealistic and inadmissible in the public realm"[16] suddenly move into the center of her reconceptualization of political theory? Since the time of its formulation, Arendt's concept of forgiveness has served as a well-established point of reference not only for philosophers such as Paul Ricoeur and Vladimir Jankélévitch,[17] but for a variety of political controversies as well: Arendt's interpretation of forgiveness played a role in the discussions of the South African Truth and Reconciliation Commission in the 1990s and, more recently, in the debate about amnesty for the imprisoned, confessed members of the Red Army Faction in Germany.[18]

1950 — PARDON DENIED

In the very first entry in her *Denktagebuch* in June 1950, Arendt wrote,

> radical evil is what should not have happened, i.e., something with which we cannot be reconciled, something we cannot under any circumstances accept as fate or an act of God, and also something we must not pass by in silence.... Revenge and forgiveness can punish it, but since they assume the sinful nature of man, i.e., that it is possible for anyone to have committed any crime, they actually cannot pass judgment on it."[19]

Radical evil could not be accepted, yet in Germany she saw people whispering and pursuing their daily lives in silence about the past. Back in New York, Arendt formulated this intellectual and moral dilemma as the first entry in her *Denktagebuch*. She clearly distinguishes between God and man, who are coupled together in the Christian idea of brotherly love. "The wrong someone has committed is a weight on their shoulders, something they carry because they have burdened themselves with it.... Only God" can relieve them of it.[20] Forgiveness, she continues, exists only between people who are qualitatively different from one other. Thus parents can forgive their children as long as the children are young, because the parents are their absolute superiors. Between equals, the gesture of forgiveness destroys the foundation of human interaction so radically that after such an act, there can basically no longer be a relationship. To forgive someone can mean only to forgo taking revenge, to pass by in silence, and that is a fundamental leave-taking, "while revenge always remains close to the other person and does not sever the relationship."[21]

Revenge "remains close to the other person" because people manifest themselves to each other in speech and action. That is, even in their mistakes and misdeeds, people are people and form relationships. In the same entry, Arendt went even further to say that forgiveness between equals was a "sham event."[22] The burden someone has put on his own shoulders is apparently lifted, while the other, the forgiving person, must accept a burden and at the same time appear to be "unburdened," to *rise* above the other and his misdeed. Only thus can the wrongdoer be unburdened of his wrong action. No one, Arendt wrote, can be that unburdened.

For Arendt in 1950, forgiveness between two people can be grounded only in the Christian solidarity of sinfulness.[23] She does not explicitly mention the temporal dimension of revenge and forgiveness that Friedrich Nietzsche spoke of. Revenge—which, according to Nietzsche, is "the Will's repugnance for Time and its 'it was'"[24]—says that our present is still under the cloud of misdeeds in the past, but forgiveness allows the present to walk away and leave the past behind. For this reason as well, forgiveness in 1950 was politically unthinkable.

The Christian concept of forgiveness was unusable, but an alternative was not then in sight. There must have been some precipitating event, some affliction that provided the impetus for her to rethink and reinvigorate the concept. For by the time Arendt had written *The Human Condition*, she had unlearned the concept in its Christian context and relearned it in the context of the political, making promise and forgiveness the guarantors of political freedom.

1953 — ONCE A COMMUNIST, NOT ALWAYS A COMMUNIST

In the *Denktagebuch* we can follow the traces of the path of this unlearning. We come upon the next entry on the concept of forgiveness in 1953.[25] At the peak of the McCarthy era, she writes that forgiveness, like pity and reconciliation, marks a new beginning in an action that is already under way. Senator Joseph McCarthy's witch hunt against former Communists and Communist sympathizers threatened Arendt and Heinrich Blücher both politically and personally. Anyone who had come into contact with Communist movements or related organizations during the 1920s and 1930s would be targeted unless they were willing to cooperate with the House Committee on Un-American Activities and its chairman's aggressive anticommunism. Former Communists and others only suspected or accused of being such were persecuted although they had done nothing wrong.

Even if they had only sympathized with organizations on the left, actors, factory workers, directors, writers, bank employees, and others were subpoenaed by the committee and expected to contritely, humbly, and publicly renounce their previous associations and voluntarily denounce former comrades or fellow travelers. On the basis of earlier political beliefs, many people in 1950, including quite a few émigrés, had already been arrested, fired from their jobs, or forbidden to publish or perform. Even the Nobel laureate Thomas Mann was attacked as a Communist sympathizer; he left the country in 1951.

———

Hannah Arendt had become a U.S. citizen in 1951, Heinrich Blücher in 1952. Because of his former membership in the illegal military wing of the German Communist party, Blücher's teaching position at Bard College was endangered. Worse, under McCarthy he was threatened with loss of citizenship, since ten thousand naturalizations were being "reviewed" in 1953.[26] It reminded Arendt and many other émigrés of the policies of the Nazis, which is why she called for defining the forced revocation of citizenship as a crime against humanity.

More disturbing than the politics of the American right, which they abhorred, were the aggressive agitation and propaganda practiced by some apostate leftists. Arendt and Blücher were not the only ones to discern totalitarian features in the American struggle against totalitarianism. McCarthy's logic that the end (containment of Stalinism) justified the means (undemocratic policies) barely got challenged in public discussion. McCarthy pursued a double strategy: within the United States he aimed to weaken the left, while in Europe he courted economic, political, and cultural leaders in order to bind the neutral countries to the West and unite them against the Soviet Union under the watchwords "freedom" and "democracy." Arendt's opposition was aroused by people who had once been Communists and with whom she thought she was in partial agreement in the critique of totalitarian aspects of Stalinism. Now they were appearing as star witnesses for McCarthy. This was a phenomenon she needed to think through!

In an article titled "The Ex-Communists," she analyzed how these McCarthy loyalists had simply switched allegiances. Instead of demanding communism as they had earlier, they now called for unconditional loyalty and cooperation in denouncing others for the sake of freedom and democracy. They still had a cause, just a different one from before. The new cause, the right cause, she continued, had a totalitarian catch to it.

By turning democracy "into a cause,"[27] something that would arrive in the future and to which the present must be devoted, the present became unfree. The idea of futurity destroyed the present moment.[28]

How could one escape this destruction of the present by fear of the future, to say nothing of McCarthy's motto "once a Communist, always a Communist," according to which one could never leave one's past behind but was condemned to continue along the path of one's former convictions and actions? It could not be right that Heinrich Blücher's years of advocacy for Soviet Russia and silence about its tyranny would define and follow him for the rest of his life, despite the insight he had gained in the meantime into the nature of totalitarianism.

The central analyses of forgiving and promising in *The Human Condition* suggest that already by 1953, Arendt may have been asking herself how a former Communist could prevent himself from being shackled to "one single deed" for his entire life. Because of the fact of his earlier membership in the party, Heinrich Blücher might "remain the victim of its consequences forever, not unlike the sorcerer's apprentice who lacked the magic formula to break the spell,"[29] a prisoner of his own deeds.

———

What troubled her in 1953 was how many friends cooperated with McCarthy. Apostates from communism let themselves be reduced to cogs in the senator's propaganda machine, among them a whole list of former friends and colleagues such as Ignazio Silone, Clement Greenberg and Elliot Cohen (with both of whom Arendt had worked), Sidney Hook, Harold Rosenberg, and also Varian Fry, who had founded the network in Marseille that smuggled many refugees, including Arendt and Blücher, to America. After the war, he too danced to McCarthy's tune even though—or perhaps because—he himself stood accused of being a Communist. After the proceeding against him was dropped, he said, "It was right that I should suffer...if our society can be safe."[30]

Like philistines, these converts now marched under the banner of precisely the (conservative) slogans of "freedom and democracy" from whose inner emptiness and spuriousness they had fled into the leftist movement in the first place during the New Deal.[31] Out of whatever fear they felt, these apostates allowed themselves to be co-opted by those in power. In a letter to a friend in Germany, Hannah Arendt wrote that they were attempting "to condition man and to adjust him to society (whatever that may mean)," and she continued in German, *"Hier schaltet sich Hinz an Kunz und Kunz an Hinz gleich."*[32]

While Ignazio Silone wrote of a "final conflict...between the Communists and ex-Communists," Arendt and Blücher felt increasingly isolated. "I'm doing all right, but am more and more losing contact with most people here—partly for reasons of politics (the McCarthy business is quite serious and the differences are very deep)," she wrote to Gershom Scholem.[33] And Alfred Kazin noted in his memoirs, "As the McCarthyite epidemic grew and Hannah in public mocked ex-Communists who became heresy hunters and professional patriots, the Bluechers came to think of themselves as a lonely wagon train fighting off the redskins."[34]

In about 1950, Arendt gave a lecture with the enigmatic title "The Eggs Speak Up," explained by the epigraph she chose from "A War" by Randall Jarrell:

There set out, slowly, for a Different World,

At four, on winter mornings, different legs ...

You can't break eggs without making an omelette

—That's what they tell the eggs.

Jarrell had read in *Origins* that totalitarianism forged a "chain of fatality"—a chain of logical arguments—which threatens to "suppress men from the history of the human race."[35] Jarrell's poem reads like a response to this sentence since it is about the necessity of interrupting this chain. With this epigraph, Arendt introduces her listeners to what she has to say. A large and varied group ("different legs") marches off on a winter morning. No head, no belly. Only the legs have set off into a different, better world. But what promised to be a better world is revealed by the title to be a war. The legs are marching in a war of ideologies that has superceded the contest of ideas.

The inspiration for the poem was the news from an American source that Stalin had commented on the famine in the Ukraine—artificially produced, as we now know—with the sarcastic proverb, "You can't make an omelet without breaking eggs." Arendt's friend Jarrell had turned Stalin's homey folk wisdom on its head: "You can't break eggs without making an omelette." With a single line, the poet conjured an image that expressed the twentieth century's perversion of common sense into murderous nonsense. Don't think! Just keep marching in the knowledge that your sacrifice will ensure a good outcome! Jarrell's image unmasks Stalin's cynicism, and its continuation in the next line is completely in the spirit of Arendt's critique of totalitarianism: "That's what they tell the eggs." Who was this "they"? And who were the eggs? In the original proverb, the process is abstract, a sort of law of nature, something that happens independent of human will and action, something we can understand only passively. But the last line reconnects the abstract figure of speech with human action and participation. The rulers "tell" and the eggs can hear what they say, which restores the idea that they can also contradict what they hear. In an age of totalitarian movements, an age subject to factual constraints, dominated by the logic of machines, and threatened by nuclear war, Jarrell has given new life to the dimensions of experience and action. By using this as her epigraph, Arendt makes it known that the proverb about eggs and omelettes is a declaration of war against humanity, that a language governed by catchwords, clichés, and commonplaces must be broken open, and that what is at stake is to recover the dimension of action and plant it in the mind of her hearers.

————

This epigraph points the way to Arendt's dialogue with poetry. For art contains the possibility of restoring the connection to the world that has been severed by totalitarianism. Through the act of trans-porting, trans-lating them into fiction, artists are able to keep alive concepts, thoughts, and ideas that have lost their presence in the world. Concepts and ideas that have become dubious can be reexamined through art. It was this never-ending work on the theoretical foundations that inspired the dialogue between Arendt and the poets.[36]

Arendt thought that the only people who still believed in the world were artists. For her, the persistence of works of art reflected the persistent character of the world. Artists could not afford to be alienated from it. With the epigraph from Jarrell, she brought the wisdom of poetry into her work of comprehension. In an age of loss of authority and a break with tradition, metaphors are points of access where the philosopher can approach what Hans Blumenberg calls the "substructures" of concepts. Poets need to explain to themselves the disturbances and concerns that the world confronts them with and preserve them in images, especially when the questions have become too loud and the foundations too weak.

―――――

Literature destabilizes thought by breaking open language and smuggling in sound, rhythm, and image―an invasion of aesthetics. More easily than analytic writing, poetry can emancipate itself from the standard definitions of words, enabling a breakthrough to new (and perhaps wayward or even nonsensical) meaning, which can then develop *after the fact*―different at each new reading. Literary language is presumptuous. It dips into the unknown in order to get nearer to a truth different from that of the superficially visible. As the poet Franz Josef Czernin described it, it is as though one step after another into emptiness could become a ladder. Literary writing can take the writers themselves by surprise; it can disturb and disappoint them―for stirring up turmoil is inherent in metaphor. Thus with every flash of understanding that comes from hearing or reading a poem, the fundamental work of thinking is taken up anew.

Jarrell's poem had opened a space of associations for Arendt that she continued to explore in "Ideology and Terror," the final chapter of *The Origins of Totalitarianism*, in which she treats more explicitly the reign of clichés. To thinking in clichés, which she would address again in her portrait of Eichmann,[37] Arendt opposed the "reality of experience,"[38] the intellectual encounter and engagement with the real world as it exists. Blücher, with his Communist past, refused to be slotted into the list of anticommunists. In the early 1950s, he resisted classification as either a Communist or an ex-Communist. To extend the metaphor of the omelette, he wanted to stop being thought of as an egg. Above all, it was crucial to stop thinking of oneself as an egg willing to be broken for a supposedly good cause. Thinking like an egg threatened everyone's freedom. Arendt had written in her *Denktagebuch* in 1950, "If someone has already concluded that 'you can't plane a board without making shavings,' his friends can no longer dissuade him, for he's already decided not to have any. He's sacrificed them all. Nothing but shavings."[39]

Platitudes must not be allowed to carry the day! In Arendt's view, McCarthy's aim—to fend off the Russian threat—did not justify the means. An evil deed brings evil into the world no matter how lofty its intentions.

In 1953, Arendt not only formulated the possibility of intervention in an action already under way in order to begin it anew but also emphasized that forgiveness, pity, and reconciliation do not "undo anything. Rather, they carry forward the action that has begun, but in a direction that was not inherent to it."[40] These words contain the germ of the great significance forgiveness would have for political freedom in *The Human Condition*. She expressed herself similarly in the lectures on Marx that she was giving at the same time in Princeton: "The experience of doing and forgiving is one, that is the knowledge that whoever does must be ready to forgive and whoever forgives actually does."[41]

It was impossible to reverse history, even one's own. Deeds could not be undone, but one could carry one's own history forward "in a direction that was not inherent to it." Our own deeds must not be allowed to pursue us forever. The idea that our ability to forgive, to take pity, and to be reconciled creates freedom for action had entered the world. But for now, that was as far as it went.

Unlike in the Marx lecture, the concept of forgiveness does not occur in "The Eggs Speak Up." Nor did Arendt develop any new idea of forgiveness in her essay that same year on the ex-Communists, although she did call for establishing "friendship wherever we can, and this goes for former Fascists or Nazis as well as going for former Communists and Bolshevists"[42]—the idea of a return to the community for former Nazis and Communists who had not committed any crimes. The friendship she means is not Christian and private. It is a political friendship. It does not appeal to the idea that all humans—including oneself—are sinners. Friendship means recognition of plurality and the possibility of a change of mind. Such friendship, perhaps originating in the solidarity of mankind against nature, is a prelude to Arendt's later political conception of forgiveness.

1958 — FREEDOM AND CHANGE OF MIND

After suggesting in her lectures on Marx that action and forgiveness, "the experience of doing and forgiving," are one, she took the next step in *The Human Condition*. In an early entry in the *Denktagebuch*, she wrote, "Nietzsche: we will keep the promise that life has made to us."[43] Here Arendt articulates her notion of the covenant each of us enters into with life by virtue of being born, providing that we are able to "make the present actual" and not allow ourselves to be "consumed" by the powers of the past or the future.[44] The ability to forgive and the ability to promise are the human characteristics that guarantee our freedom from being ruled by the past or the future. If forgiveness and forgetting did not exist, every past action would be irrevocable and the present would be dominated by the past. If promising did not exist, the entire future would be unforeseeable and the present would be dominated by all the fears and uncertainties of the future. Arendt argues implicitly against Nietzsche's thesis in *On the Genealogy of Morality* that man must be forced into equality by the threat of punishment and be "reared" to keep his promises. In other words, he must put on the "social straightjacket" to reduce his fear. In the *Denktagebuch*, Arendt argues that only a mutual promise, freely given, can unite men by binding them together, and it is when men autonomously recall the premises of their binding, willed decision, thus "vouching for the future," that they feel themselves to be voluntarily committed to their own "memory of the will."[45] Against the danger of becoming a prisoner of either one's previous deeds or one's fears, the ability to forgive and to promise heralds the "glad tidings"[46] of the possibility of a new beginning in freedom.

In rethinking the concept of forgiveness, Hannah Arendt set out to follow the path blazed by Walter Benjamin, Martin Buber, Martin Heidegger, and Franz Rosenzweig in search of the original experience of forgiveness. In order to reach the root meaning of the word, to peel back "what had become of the words over the centuries"[47] and strip off their abstract theological or philosophical accretions, Arendt returned to the biblical sources. "The discoverer of the role of forgiveness in the realm of human affairs was Jesus of Nazareth."[48] She quotes Luke 17:4 from the King James Bible: "And if he trespass against thee seven times [in] a day, and seven times in a day turn again to thee, saying, I repent; thou shalt forgive him."[49]

In fact, as Arendt points out in a footnote, in the original Greek there are additional connotations that the translation cannot fully encompass: "The verse which I quote in the standard translation could also be rendered as follows: 'And if he trespass against thee...and...turn again to thee, saying, *I changed my mind*; thou shalt *release* him.'"[50]

By thus returning to the source and rereading the ancient text, the (primal) experience behind the concept can be regained and reinvigorated. According to the source, the only one who can forgive is the person who has been wronged. Moreover, forgiveness demands a dialogue, including specifically the expression of a change of mind on the part of the one who has done wrong. And finally, forgiveness concludes by "releasing" the offender, granting him the freedom to make a new beginning. Remorse, the wish that something had not happened, is for Arendt an impossibility, for it is precisely our incapacity to undo our actions that, in her eyes, guarantees human existence and reaffirms that we have truly been alive. According to Arendt, with a change of mind the wrongdoer proves nothing less than that he is, here and now, a different person. The idea of a new moment in which the participants can become different people than they were in the past is a recognition of doing and forgiving as acts of free will, which—assuming a change of mind—forgives the deed and thus grants freedom to both sides.

The human ability to forgive, Arendt wrote in *The Human Condition*, is not only a matter between two individuals but is also and especially indispensable as a political "remedy."[51] Life could simply not go on if people were not constantly releasing each other from the consequences of what they had done. Such forgiveness, in contrast to the one-sided devotion of brotherly love, offers the possibility that a deed can cease having consequences.

For eight long pages in *The Human Condition*, Hannah Arendt struggled with words, seeking to get closer to the rationale and the necessity for the concept of forgiveness, but also to its flaws. Forgiveness, she wrote, is no longer an act of divine will but completely of this world. Nor is it unconditional; it can occur only under the condition that the wrongdoer has asked for forgiveness and desires a new beginning:

> Only through this constant mutual release from what they do can men remain free agents, only by constant willingness to change their minds and start again can they be trusted with so great a power as that to begin something new.[52]

Translated into the political realm, what is needed is mutual agreement to that change of mind; people must be willing to change their minds so they can be "trusted" to begin something new. And they need a reliable place where this can occur. A constitution and laws are, for Arendt, the guarantors of that place.

———

Arendt's new political conceptions of forgiveness and promise are from now on carried by the idea, further developed in *On Revolution* (1963), that nations or republics (which in everyday life are fragmented conglomerations of the poor, the rich, the sick, the depressed, the unemployed, bureaucrats, actors, and florists), through the declaration of will embodied in their founding act (and based on these notions of promise and forgiveness), can develop the power to bring foreign or even formerly inimical peoples into "participation with each other."

Yet forgiveness remains an act that cannot be decreed. The supplicant has no means of demanding pardon and must at every moment be prepared for the possibility of failure. His only, fragile hope lies in the feeling that our shared humanity is stronger than the deed that divides us. Freedom is a "great power" that cannot be had without the danger of failure, since the person who asks forgiveness knows that it is possible that he will remain unforgiven. The possible encounter with not being forgiven and the knowledge of the existence of the unforgivable are inherent in the concrete plea for forgiveness. Moreover, forgiveness is not an act of the will, no matter how logical forgiving someone seems and no matter how earnest the resolve to forgive. There is always something that remains. You cannot depend on logic or a decision to forgive. There is more at play, an interpersonal remainder. Forgiveness is hostile to the supremacy of reason. Small wonder that in the course of the Enlightenment, it was delegated to Christianity.

1961 — THE COVENANT

Between 1950 and 1958, we find that Arendt had unlearned her traditional ideas. She had learned that to connect forgiveness to notions such as divine grace or brotherly love was a hindrance (in Deleuze's sense of the word). The turbulent times had unsettled her and forced her to rethink the concept. We can also discern the impulse in her engagement with the disruptive power of poetry, so essential for the unlearning of a concept.

At one point in *Vita activa*, Arendt elaborated her notion of forgiveness. In the English version, the wrong is forgiven for the sake of the person. In the German version, however, the person is forgiven for the sake of humanity, while the deed itself remains almost ignored in the process of forgiving. It is not forgotten; it remains. But if forgiveness has taken place, the wrong that was committed no longer stands between the parties involved.

One of the influences on Arendt's shift of emphasis between *The Human Condition* and *Vita activa* may have been the dialogue with her friend W. H. Auden. We don't know the content of their conversations, but some traces of them remain in their writings and other references. Auden initially responded to Arendt's new definition of forgiveness in *The Human Condition* with a review[53] as well as in an essay on Shakespeare.[54] (After reading the latter, Arendt wrote to him, "I just read your Falstaff piece.") In the essay, Auden elaborated and reinforced the power and authority of brotherly love and humanity's duty to do good to one another. Without these virtues, any notion of forgiveness would be dominated by dependence, whereas if one forgave out of love for one's fellow man, no one would be dependent on another—instead, you could say that we are all in one another's good graces. Auden's objection was that Arendt's notion of forgiveness delivered the wrongdoer into the power of the forgiver. Such power over the person asking forgiveness contained the danger that the wrongdoer would be humiliated or insulted. It was a fundamental objection. Moreover, he rejected Hannah Arendt's idea that forgiveness is tied to conditions. According to Auden, forgiving obeys the commandment to love one another, a commandment that is "unconditional" and therefore absolute. Arendt answered in a letter:

> You talk about charity as though it were love, and it is true that
> love will forgive everything because of its utter commitment to

the beloved person. But even love violates the integrity of the wrongdoer if it forgives without having been asked to. Is not forgiving without being asked to really impertinent, or at least conceited—as though one said: Much as you tried, you could not wrong me; charity has made me invulnerable?... I do not know what is more difficult: to demand a coat or to give the cloak also, but I am quite sure that it is more difficult to ask than to give forgiveness. This side of the matter, that is, the mutuality of the whole business, remains outside all considerations in "doing good," but it is essential for the act of forgiving.

In the same letter, Arendt formulated her change of mind:

I was wrong when I said that we forgive what was done for the sake of who did it. I may forgive somebody who betrayed me but I am not going to condone betrayal überhaupt [entirely, completely]. I can forgive somebody without forgiving anything.... But charity indeed forgives überhaupt, it forgives betrayal in the person who betrayed—on the ground, to be sure, of human sinfulness and its solidarity with the sinner.[55]

Thus Arendt criticizes the fact that charity or brotherly love is a mixture of humility and arrogance, humility that insists that we are all sinners, and arrogance that, in the end, insists that the judgment of the other person remains, in effect, silent and unchangeable.

Unlike the purely personal dimension of forgiveness, the political dimension in *Vita activa* is based on respect or, as Arendt calls it, "political friendship." Forgiveness does not ask after benefit or advantage, talents or defects; it rests on no judgment nor is it an appeal from a judgment. It is not earned. It is founded only on the fact that human beings wish to retain for themselves and others their respect for what is humane in the human being, for the human ability to make a new beginning. This respect is Arendt's escape from the Christian "solidarity with the sinner."

———

By 1961, Hannah Arendt's public analysis of the concept of forgiveness had reached its conclusion. Forgiveness is a sort of political covenant that robs a wrong of its future effectiveness without forgetting it. The results of forgiveness, like the results of all actions, are free and unforeseeable. The German version, even more than the English version, is saturated with the idea that this world is one we share. "Closed within ourselves, we would never be able to forgive ourselves any failing or transgression because we would lack the experience of the person for the sake of whom one can forgive."[56] Thus ends the section on forgiveness. But it ended nothing. Instead of providing solutions, it left unanswered questions: What happens politically with deeds that are unpunishable and unforgivable? Where does the wrong that has been done go if it doesn't vanish from the world upon its doer being forgiven? Can it really cease to have consequences? Wouldn't that be a miracle of some kind?

BENNO VON WIESE

On October 17, 1953, Benno von Wiese, a professor of German and a friend of Hannah Arendt's from her student days, wrote, "Although I know from Hugo Friedrich that you don't want to have much to do with me anymore, I'm writing all the same since I think that you should be reconciled with me just like Richard Alewyn has been in the meantime.... Do you really intend to cease all possible 'communication' between us forever?" And he added in a postscript, "Do you think Heidegger deserves to meet with you again more than I do?" Arendt replied in a letter that has not survived but was clearly not unfriendly, since Benno von Wiese's next letter began, "Yesterday's letter from you was really a great joy," since it had been possible to bridge "the inner and outer gulf of years and decades" in an apparent reconciliation.[57]

As a student, Benno von Wiese had had an affair with the Jew Hannah Arendt, and now he spoke to her of a "gulf." What he meant was his career under the National Socialist regime. He had joined the party in 1933, was named an associate professor in 1936, and was declared "indispensable" during the war and exempted from military service. In 1945, after going through denazification, he was able to resume his academic career. In 1953 he reestablished contact with Hannah Arendt, but in 1964 the gulf between them opened again. Both Bonn University where von Wiese taught and the Germanistenverband, the association of professors of German, had come under criticism for having been eager to cooperate with the National Socialists. In an essay in the prestigious weekly newspaper *Die Zeit* titled "Remarks on the Unmastered Past," Benno von Wiese wrote about his own complicity: "No one likes to admit that he has been mistaken or even has done something wrong.... Remembering the past...cannot mean that an entire generation of people who in the meantime have been working as public employees is now to be pilloried."[58] In his opinion, he didn't deserve that. Hannah Arendt found some of the phrases he used particularly shocking: "We succumbed to the spirit of the times" and "The spirit [*Geist*] of the times revealed itself more and more to be a demon [*Ungeist*]." He hadn't succumbed to the spirit of the times, she wrote him on December 25, 1964. Instead—and sooner than many others—he had succumbed to his fear for his "public career."

Concretely, she reproached him for urging as early as 1933 "the 'removal of alien blood' from the universities." "Whom did you know back then with alien blood in their veins?" she asked, and answered laconically, "me, whom you had counted among your best friends only a few months earlier."[59]

Arendt and von Wiese had met several times after 1953 and he made several unsuccessful attempts—from whatever impulse—to recruit her as an expert on Kafka and Brecht to write an essay for one of his collections of articles on German literature. But his essay in *Die Zeit* and the exchange of letters that followed revealed that the gulf that separated them because of his past actions had not closed after all. In Arendt's eyes, however, it was not merely a gulf in their personal relationship; it had a political dimension as well.

> It's not true that you succumbed to the spirit of the times in the person of Hitler. What is true is that you succumbed to the fear of that certainly very frightening spirit. Those are two different things. Because you foolishly did not want to admit your own fear, you then compounded the misfortune by succumbing to the spirit of the times after all. Now first of all, your fear was so justified that it would be foolish to hold it against you. But the second thing is different. Nothing was further from my mind than to condemn you. I only wanted to reason with you and it seems to me that for you as a person it would have been better if in the past you had admitted to yourself—not to anyone else—that

you were acting from fear and not from conviction. In that case, the conviction would never have come and you would have seen more clearly how far you had to go and what you had no need to say or to print. You would have kept your judgment. And as far as the present is concerned, it seems to me smarter to say to young people "We were afraid" than to implicitly admit "We were stupid" and then to expect people to pardon and explain away your nonsense as past history. It's clear that the younger generation can read and that what you and others like you wrote back then sounds comical not only to present-day ears. ("Hearing the speeches that ring from your house, one laughs./But whoever sees you, reaches for his knife." Brecht wrote that in the thirties.) Anyone can understand this much: that it was nonsense both then and now, without needing to call on a "sense of history." But the fear that drove you to that nonsense is indeed much harder to understand. When you write that "we succumbed to the spirit of the times" it sounds very nice as long as one forgets that Hitler, who looked like a con artist and not like a Napoleon, was the embodiment of that spirit. I fear you've forgotten that. At any rate, in your place I would ten thousand times rather admit that I was afraid than that I fell for that nonsense on my own initiative and without any other motives. God knows I had no wish to condemn you, and when we made up in New York I knew all that and meant what I said.

And now I'll bring this to a close. I was irritated. And it's still my opinion that you haven't ever thought these things through clearly, and that it's better for you to keep your mouth shut when you have no clarity. The fact that you're not the only one with this attitude is no excuse. But it does explain why the "alienation" between the generations could become so great. You and people like you, it seems to me, failed twice to do the right thing, not just under Hitler, but especially thereafter.[60]

Our deeds remain. They are not forgotten, but they should no longer stand between us.

THE TASK OF UNLEARNING

At the end of the unlearning we have outlined, it is clear that a thought, like a poem, is never finished but rather, in Jorge Luis Borges's words, "relinquished," given over to the life to come and its influence upon it. This was also true of Arendt's groundwork for a new foundation of forgiving. The French philosopher Paul Ricoeur—who was seven years younger than Hannah Arendt and read Jaspers and translated Husserl while a prisoner of war in Germany—met Arendt in the early 1970s at the New School in New York. Like many philosophers, he took up the ideas Arendt had given birth to and continued to elaborate on them in his own way. Like Walter Benjamin, Ricoeur sees it as the historian's task to salvage possibilities for action that have been forgotten and to liberate the unkept promises of the past from the ruins of history. Drawing on Arendt's notions of historical reflection in his essay "The Riddle of the Past," Ricoeur describes two particular dangers when dealing with what has preceded us: escapist forgetting or endless obsession. In the case of what he calls "difficult forgiveness," by which he means forgiving grave crimes, it is still necessary for forgiveness to border on forgetting, "not forgetting the facts," which are truly inextinguishable, but forgetting their significance for the present and future.

In the difficult work of unlearning, Arendt drove out her own "opinions" on the concept of forgiveness—as in many previous cases, she "forgot" the unexamined prejudices that keep us from thinking.[61]

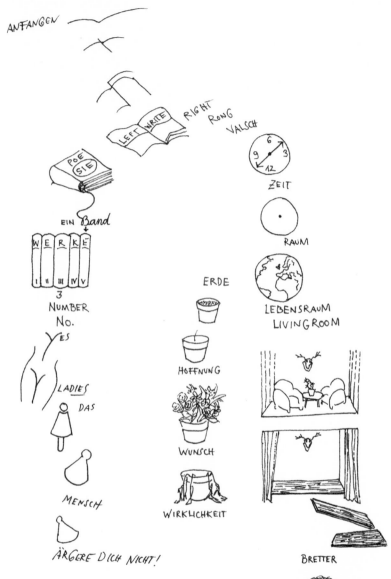

ANFANGEN

LEFT WRITE RIGHT RONG VALSCH

POE SIE

EIN Band

W E R K E
I II III IV V

3
NUMBER
No.

Yes

LADIES

DAS

MENSCH

ÄRGERE DICH NICHT!

ZEIT

RAUM

ERDE

HOFFNUNG

WUNSCH

WIRKLICHKEIT

LEBENSRAUM
LIVINGROOM

BRETTER

DIE DIE WELT BEDEUTEN

DRAMATIZATION: THE WORLD AS STAGE, THE TEXT AS SPACE

> *Citar es citarse.*
> A quote is an encounter.
> —Julio Cortázar

In W. H. Auden's essay "The Fallen City," which he wrote shortly after reading *The Human Condition*, the poet implicitly objected to Hannah Arendt's new conception of forgiveness. Auden was fascinated by the idea that forgiving is an action rather than a reaction, since the consequences of both forgiving and acting are unforeseeable. But he found Arendt's notion that the action of forgiving requires a request for forgiveness literally too dramatic. "On the stage...it is impossible to show one person forgiving another, unless the wrongdoer ask for forgiveness, because silence and inaction are undramatic."[1] On the stage, forgiveness that is not verbalized requires a clear gesture. When a good ruler like Duke Vincentio grants freedom to the bad and lawless Angelo at the end of *Measure for Measure*, we expect two things, writes Auden: a gesture that lets us know if Angelo has had a change of heart and a gesture that gives us a sense of whether the good duke is pardoning him because he really forgives him deep down, or only for the sake of his daughter.

Onstage there is always a dramatic dilemma: if not articulated in speech, both the request for forgiveness and the decision to forgive must be acted out in gestures or shown by other means, or they must be explicitly left open. Auden argues that in real life, no verbalization is required since there is an agreed-upon charity (*agape*) that needs no manifestation. It is always there, always in force.

In this almost incidental passage, Auden implicitly refers to the dramatic dimension of Arendt's political theory that we recognize in her metaphor of the world as a stage: "In acting and speaking, men show who they are, reveal actively their unique personal identities and thus make their appearance in the human world."[2] Later in the same work, she writes of the Greek polis that "it assures the mortal actor that his passing existence and fleeting greatness will never lack the reality that comes from being seen, being heard, and, generally, appearing before an audience of fellow men."[3] By being born, man makes his entrance and interrupts the course of events. Just as an actor needs a reliable place, a stage, colleagues, and an audience, every living being needs "a timeless region, an eternal presence"[4] for his entrance and other beings who acknowledge and validate his existence.

These recurring theatrical metaphors of stage, actor, and audience carry within them the question of why we are here, in the midst of all things nonhuman—the course of nature, the progress of history—and in the midst of things that are here simply in and of themselves, running along independent of us, beyond good and evil.[5] There are things that are extrahuman, but we are creatures of this world in which "everything here seems to need us, these fleeting things that/touch us strangely."[6] It is as if with her image of the world as a stage and life as an "appearance" or "entrance," Arendt had found an answer to Rilke's complaint about the "echolessness" of modern man, which she discussed in one of her early articles.[7]

Just as every spoken word is an interruption and a positing, and just as an action in Arendt's theory is capable of striking from the moment the sparks contained within it, so every person by making an entrance onto the "boards that signify the world"[8] possesses the ability to interrupt the course of nature and history, whose future would otherwise be eternally predetermined. All depends on the individual to the extent that he inserts himself into human affairs, interrupts the course of things and the way the world runs, and thus suspends the predictability of the future.

Drawing a distinction between herself and Martin Heidegger, Hannah Arendt emphasized that man is not "thrown" into the world but rather *onto the earth*, since to begin with, he is born. Only later does he then appear *in the world*, able to manifest himself in speech and action and construct the world as his home on earth.[9] Through his existence in the world, she says—again in contradistinction to Heidegger—man liberates himself from being only himself. As much as Arendt shared the existentialist distinction between facticity and existentiality—between *having* to exist and being *able* to exist—what is at stake here is the constitution of a concept of the world that is different from Heidegger's "The light of the public darkens everything" and from Rilke's "Nowhere . . . will there be world except within."[10]

Picking up on Heidegger's assertion that man lives in the "habitation" of language,[11] that language is the "house of being," as he writes in his Letter on Humanism,[12] she emphasizes the special ability of speech to create a "between." World arises *between* people, thus completely *outside of* man. Politics is the constantly renewed attempt to realize the world through the agreement of the many. Even mental activities in her view are not a withdrawal from the world but rather a withdrawal "from the world's being present to the senses."[13]

With her metaphor of the stage, Arendt does not intend to suggest that there is a predetermined script that is being produced and actors who learn and perform the play according to a preexisting plan. Unlike Plato's conception of the world as a "tragedy and comedy of life," man for Arendt is no "puppet of the gods." He is not moved by "cords and strings, which pull us different and opposite ways, and to opposite actions," making possible a (relative) freedom that always remains tied to its relation to the divinity. Nor did she have in mind Shakespeare's idea from *As You Like It* that "All the world's a stage, and all the men and women merely players." Shakespeare did not believe in a divine providence in whose reflection man seeks salvation. Instead, as his dramatic device of the play within the play shows, he was interested in the dissolution of a unified image of the world. He made it clear that the dramatic fiction is not able to encompass the entire world. And so his image includes the idea that the world is more than just everything that is the case.

SAYING THE NEW

Arendt's re-actualization of the image of the world as a stage in her writings should not be seen as a secular continuation or translation of the Greeks or a continuation of Shakespeare's play within the play. Instead, as a thinker after the rupture in tradition, she breaks open and salvages the traditional figure of thought and concludes that it has quite new and different things to say to us today. She unlearned it.

In his actions, modern man knows himself not to be empowered or intended by any god and is no longer illuminated by the light of any tradition. He must empower himself and painstakingly construct what Peter Sloterdijk calls "a message that appeals in and of itself."[14] He must avoid becoming entangled in new "cords and strings," must not have any new gods or allow himself to be guided by fixed worldviews or rely on other "banisters" such as logic or the constraints of practical existence. He must not fall under the spell of some future utopia. Instead, he must *reveal his personal uniqueness*, a self-empowerment that Arendt calls "appearing" or "having really existed." Not in existence but only in having really existed do we interrupt the linear course of time and strike from existence the sparks of the moment. Arendt's secularized and antiteleological message is that through his "presence,"[15] that is, by the fact that he realizes the present, man can disrupt what Walter Benjamin called "the continuum of history."[16]

It is no surprise that she also sees the Greek polis as a stage, a place that guaranteed the reliability Arendt regarded as fundamental through the territorial enclosure of the city walls and the intellectual content of the law. Everyone was able to be in turn both audience and contributing actor. The organization of the "audience" made it possible for the "performances" of mortal men not to disappear from this earthly reality.[17] Arendt the theoretician admired the "delight in action" and "the confidence in one's own power to change things" in the idea of the polis, and she admired the same things in the student movements of the 1960s.[18] But Hannah Arendt never had in mind Lenin's cook

("Any cook should be able to run the country" in the phrase attributed to him) nor any idea that politics was a form of self-expression, much less self-dramatization. With the image of the stage, she intends to reinforce the consciousness that man's ability to appear in the world is a conscious act, a performance, or, as she wrote in her Kafka essay, a miracle. For "the world, fabricated by men and constituted according to human and not natural laws, will become again part of nature, and will follow the law of ruin when man decides to become himself part of nature, a blind though accurate tool of natural laws, renouncing his supreme faculty of creating laws himself."[19] The miracle, the saving grace, lies in the human capacity to change the world and its "natural course."

"CITAR ES CITARSE"

The true art of the theater lies in its ability to stage scenes not only from contemporary life but also elements that transcend the boundaries of space and time. Onstage, men and women from bygone eras and even imaginary beings can cross our perceptual threshold and strike new sparks at the dramatic moment, as do Shakespeare's ghosts and sprites and even Hamlet's dead father. Anything is possible, and it can in fact be transported into this space by language, action, gesture, expression, and, of course, by exclusion, by what is not said and not done.

Through the use of quotations, metaphors, rhythms, and tropes, thinking and writing are (like the theater) able to let knowledge that is distant, past — and sometimes also endangered or in danger of being forgotten — make an entrance into our concern about the present. Quotations and fragments interrupt our own voice and train of thought; they people the text that is taking shape in our solitary room and intervene in the flow of ideas. Fragments of alien experience are handed down in quotations,[20] and even taken out of their original context, they still tell of the whole that is concealed behind them and ought not to be given up as lost. Yet at the same time, they clearly reject the ideal of a whole, which is apparent through their own intrusive foreignness. Arendt is aware of her own state of exile, as Franz Rosenzweig formulated it, and her text cannot do without that knowledge. She cannot surrender the experience of foreignness and accept the world as something unmediated.[21]

In her 1968 portrait of her friend Walter Benjamin, Arendt connected his passion as a bibliophile to his passion as a collector of quotations, an obsession that culminated in the Arcades Project. Collecting, she wrote, is actually a preoccupation of children and people who have no need for utilitarian objects. A bibliophile's books are "liberated from the drudgery of usefulness,"[22] and that is the status of quotations as well. Benjamin's quotations, according to Arendt, prove nothing. They have no need to document an analysis or interpretation of the world, no need to shore up a logical argument. Quotations are voices the author introduces into the space of a text, voices that can encounter one another in continually new ways in the here and now of writing, just as they do in the here and now of reading. They repeatedly illuminate one another in different ways within the space of the text. The impoverished world of today, where the act of thinking is under threat of collapse, has need of "thought fragments" from the past, voices that the author brings into the space of the text and allows to associate with each other. In Arendt's texts as well, quotations are seldom used as documentation. Instead, they create a multilayered and polyphonic plurality. After the break with tradition, they protect the sources of tradition from running dry.

As she writes, it must have been Walter Benjamin's aspiration to let the author's voice disappear in the montage and to regard the text as a space that he, Benjamin, puts at the disposal of the foreign voices, which would then, with the aid of his arrangement in the montage, illuminate not just one another but also, and above all, the present moment. Unlike Benjamin, however, Arendt is extremely present as the author in her textual space. She allows her thoughts to become enmeshed in others' voices; she allows the foreign voices to be heard and takes her own stand. She judges. "The more individuals someone has within him," Nietzsche wrote, "the more he alone will have the prospect of finding a truth."[23] Above all, Arendt brings the wisdom of poetry into her texts.

> Remembrance, *Mnēmosynē*, the mother of the muses, is directly transformed into memory, and the poet's means to achieve the transformation is rhythm, through which the poem becomes fixed in the recollection almost by itself. It is this closeness to living recollection that enables the poem to remain, to retain its durability, outside the printed or the written page, and though the "quality" of a poem may be subject to a variety of standards, its "memorability" will inevitably determine its durability, that is, its chance to be permanently fixed in the recollection of humanity. Of all things of thought, poetry is closest to thought, and a poem is less a thing than any other work of art.[24]

We hear again an echo of Heidegger's notion of the "habitation of language" that concluded with the statement, "The thinkers and the poets are the guardians of this habitation." Both disciplines can dispense with material, tangible objects and the entelechies and constraints inherent in them. Like song, thinking and poetry require no paper, no pen, no canvas. Their progress is not dependent on the drying of paint.

Poetry originated "as a living spoken word in the recollection of the bard and those who listened to him."[25] And the poet's words that populate a text—words that are not mere text but almost physical bodies composed of rhythm, form, sound, compression, and contraction—are sound bodies carrying within them the fact that they have been recollected and spoken, voices that impress themselves on memory through all the senses. In the process, many quotations have gotten so firmly anchored in memory that they have become part of thought, memorized without being recognized and recalled as quotations.

In addition, metaphors from outside the poet himself—the bread of poetry—break open the writer's own language, creating a heterogeneity from which the text gains the power to relativize its own convictions and destroy its dogmas. The foreign images as well as the foreign sounds and rhythms in the text form places of meeting and zones of uncertainty. They contribute to the fact that Arendt's texts are not exhausted by one reading but are capable of an ongoing inner unfolding. Arendt adds what she has heard to what is her own. Thus arises a polyphonic, shared present that is also an aesthetic experience.

———

This resonant space was the treasure Hannah Arendt was able to extract from the great misfortune of exile. Foreign images have a special power, as one can see from the Homeric and biblical images ("eloquent in word and vigorous in deed," "as the flower of grass," etc.) in the following passage. They enable collisions:

> For a man can be "eloquent in word and vigorous in deed," but neither words nor deeds leave behind a trace in the world. Nothing bears witness to them after the brief moment in which they pass through the world like a breeze or a wind or a storm and shake the hearts of men. Without the tools that *Homo faber* designs in order to ease men's labors and shorten their hours of work, human life would be nothing but toil and effort. Without the permanence of the world that outlasts mortal man's span of life on earth, the races of man would be as grass, and all the glory of man as the flower of grass, and without the productive arts of *Homo faber*—but now at the highest level in the full glory of their purest development—without the poets and the historians, without the arts of forming and narrating, the only thing that speaking and acting men are able to produce—namely, the history in which they appear as actors and speakers until it has proceeded to the point that someone can report it as history—that history would never impress itself on the memory of man so that it became a part of the world in which men live.[26]

It is a sentence structure typical of Arendt's prose, in which repetition of an element (without…without…without) introduces clauses that open up more and more aspects of the world, aspects the author or the reader could continue to vary indefinitely. For that's how our world works, with new spaces of the imagination constantly unfolding. By calling up images from Luther's translation of the Bible ("des Grases Blüte"—the flower of the grass) in the context of common, everyday problems of working people, Arendt praises the richness and beauty of the world, confronts man's adversity (unemployment and fewer work hours), and in the same breath celebrates the world's permanence. For if we can catch the sound of these ancient words today, it means we not only have the meager present at our disposal but can also still hear what is past. We have not yet lost the world in its creation, for something the Apostle Peter knew has remained: heaven and earth must fade away, but the promise behind them is still there. "For all flesh is as grass, and all the glory of man as the flower of grass. The grass withereth, and the flower thereof falleth away: But the word of the Lord endureth for ever."[27]

Arendt's unlearning loosens both concepts and quotations from their historical moorings and traditional environments. Beyond that, Arendt's practice of quotation releases her own thinking and writing again and again from the long since discredited temptation to plow forward, logically and linearly, toward a conclusion. Her foreign images and quotations derail the forward momentum of her own train of thought. The thinkers and writers of the past are freed from their history; their words and works appear in Arendt's work and turn out to have new things to say.

OUT OF JOINT

If quotations no longer need to document things, they can turn up in new ways, appearing on the stage of various texts and revealing different things. For instance, the following lines from Hamlet:

> The time is out of joint; Oh cursèd spite
> That ever I was born to set it right![28]

We recall that Hamlet has returned to Denmark where he is mourning the death of his father the king. He has been told that his father died of a snakebite, but in reality, the king was murdered by his brother and successor, Claudius, who is also Queen Gertrude's lover. No one guesses the heinous crime and the entire court lives in the harmonious illusion of communal mourning for the dead king. The deed is so monstrous, so unimaginable, that the living do not even have language in which to conceive it. Only the ghost of Hamlet's dead father can reveal the inconceivable to him, but Hamlet cannot share what has been revealed to him with anyone. At first, he must feign madness in order to continue to live in the community, knowing the truth. A world in which the facts are unreal is a nightmare. "Being"—living in a world that faces up to the present—is confronted by "nonbeing"—a world that pretends to have assimilated with the false reality created by the murderers. Arendt knew something about that and identified this knowledge in her essay on Kafka: cast into an inhuman world, simple "men of goodwill were forced to function within it as something exceptional and abnormal—saints or madmen."[29] In *Hamlet*, it is only the traveling players whose appearance provides the impetus to "set it right" with a play within the play.

As tragic as the story of Hamlet is, his appearance on the stage of world theater and his later appearance as a quotation in a text tells of his humane attempt to resist the advance of evil—even and especially in a place where, as "in the state of Denmark," the evil deed beggars human imagination.

———

Arendt used the quote from *Hamlet* for the first time in 1954 in her lecture "Concern with Politics in Recent European Philosophical

Thought." In her heavy German accent she provided her American audience with an overview of the condition of postwar European philosophy. According to her, none of its various practitioners—Heidegger, Jaspers, Sartre, Maritain, and others—had yet really come to conceptual grips with the shock of what never should have occurred. Although they all acknowledged "the sheer horror of contemporary political events, together with the even more horrible eventualities of the future,[30] recent political experience was in fact almost absent from their analytical concepts. Arendt's lecture is a vehement plea that philosophy must turn to the deeds (and, of course, the misdeeds) of human beings and react to politics. But in fact, philosophic texts were either blind to or glossed over politics, mythologized it or fell back on old certainties, and it was a riddle how (philosophical) thought could be made fit for the new realities. It was not enough for Jaspers to praise the "unanswered soul of heroism." Maritain's Catholicism led in the end back to tradition. And French existentialism had abandoned philosophy in favor of politics, but where it was still philosophical, it had boxed itself into seeing life as absurd.

Nowhere did "political experience" enter into any of their analytical conceptualizations. They were still holding fast to tradition.

> The return to tradition ... seems to imply much more than the re-ordering of a world that is "out of joint"; it implies the re-establishment of a world that is past. And even if such an enterprise were possible, the question of which of the many worlds covered by one tradition should be re-established could be answered only in terms of arbitrary choice.

And a few pages later in the same text:

> The point is not that the present world has reached a crisis and is "out of joint," but that human existence as such is "absurd" because it presents insoluble questions to a being endowed with reason.[31]

Here, Shakespeare's "out of joint" is first of all a transatlantic metaphor that establishes a world of shared images between the native German speaker and her American audience, and, simultaneously, a space of sound, language, and imagery for the fundamental interrogation of existence via the terrors of the times in which they lived. Philosophy has not yet faced up to the metaphysical shock, she concludes. And the quote from *Hamlet* tells of the terrors of the times that resist understanding. Everything hangs in the balance: to be or not to be.

———

When Arendt uses "out of joint" a second time in the same year, the voice of Hamlet brings another aspect into her thought space. Now she includes the entire couplet from his monologue:

> In the last analysis, the human world is always the product of man's *amor mundi*, a human artifice whose potential immortality is always subject to the mortality of those who build it and the natality of those who come to live in it. What Hamlet said is always true: "The time is out of joint; O cursèd spite / That ever I was born to set it right!" In this sense, in its need for beginners that it may be begun anew, the world is always a desert.[32]

At a time dominated solely by society, "Introduction *into* Politics," from which this quotation comes, seeks a new foundation for the political to counter the "growth of worldlessness."[33]

Many outside voices here inhabit Arendt's observations on the endangered present. The voice of the writer Theodor Fontane in the lines "Tand, Tand/Ist das Gebilde von Menschenhand" (Baubles, baubles/Are the works of man)[34] whispers of the futility of all man's efforts, and Nietzsche's desert, where the windstorm of progress blows and men threaten to assimilate to society, must be kept from spreading by politics.

In "Concern with Politics in Recent European Philosophical Thought," the quotation from *Hamlet* reinforced the urgency of recognizing what was foul in the state of Denmark. In the new context of "Introduction *into* Politics," it emphasizes more strongly the necessity, indeed, the task, of humans as humans, working together to set right the time that is out of joint—the present, not Schopenhauer's world as will and representation! "Nay, come, let's go together." Thus ends Act I of *Hamlet*.

To the extent that we are human beings, Arendt asserts, we cannot live under desert conditions. If we adjust to the desert world, hope fades of a humane world made by humans. Totalitarianism threatens to set in motion the desert itself, unleashing the sandstorm over all parts of the inhabited world so that everything breaks out in "pseudo-action."[35] We are still intact and humane precisely because, like Hamlet, we *suffer* under desert conditions.

PERSONARE

Arendt uses another theatrical image, the mask of Greek tragedy, to characterize the difference between the uniqueness and instantaneousness of appearing and speaking on the one hand, and the never-ending activity of the self that is thinking on the other. While action and speech create the world, thinking is an unending dialogue "between me and myself" in which the "two" can introduce various voices, quotations, and thought fragments onto the inner stage and give them leave—thus recalled and reactualized—to go to work in her head.[36] At the moment the thinker interrupts his thought in order to appear, he remembers what he thought and puts on a mask for the moment of appearing—the mask of the single person through which his voice sounds (Latin *persona* = an actor's mask; *personare* = to sound through).[37] Thus the mask shapes the concrete form of appearing in the world. For example, no one would want to claim that courageous people know no fear; they have only decided—and that is the decisive thing—to appear fearless. And even when this appearance becomes a habit, fear would still be present. For Arendt, freedom is realized only in the concrete appearance that differs from one time to the next and disappears the moment the appearance is over. "The only person who can run the risk of appearing as one among others is the person who is prepared to exist with others in the future, and that means being prepared to move among them and give information about who one is."[38] Here again, something is unlearned: we usually assume that a mask hides the real self, but for Arendt, the mask is the form in which the self can express itself. It enables the person to turn toward the outer world. "We humanize what is going on in the world and in ourselves only by speaking of it, and in the course of speaking of it we learn to be human."[39] Thus the act of appearing puts a provisional end not only to the two-in-one of thinking but also to the idea that "inside they're all the same"[40] in the way of pure vegetative functioning. "Only what *appears* outwardly is distinct, different, even unique. In one word, our emotions are all the same, the difference is in what and how we make them appear."[41] Nature, in other words, has hidden and left formless everything that is purely functional. This act of appearing is the gamble of being a person.

THE LIVING ROOM

Arendt's work is a conversation with "friends," with Plato and Socrates, Shakespeare and Lessing, Rahel Varnhagen, Heinrich Heine, Emily Dickinson, and Rilke, as much as with her contemporaries Heidegger, Jarrell, Sarraute, Auden, McCarthy, and Broch.[42] This eros of conversation and friendship runs through her entire work and can also be discerned in her quotations. Arendt even brings together people who possibly never spoke to each other in real life, people who never would have wanted or been able to speak to each other, and these voices develop thereby an eerie power. They colonize the present of her judgment and rob that present of the "mindless peace" of simplistic, one-dimensional certainties and unthinking complacency.[43] Doors are opened and new spaces revealed.

Quotations allow others to appear in the conversational space of a written text or a speech. They establish mysterious interconnections that always carry with them nonplausibility. Fissures and areas of uncertainty arise that readers or listeners can actualize for themselves at other times and in other places, thus encouraging their own imaginations. Such blank spaces draw readers out of passive reception of what is written and encourage their participation in shaping its meaning.

———

In a long poem titled "A Living Room," Theodore Weiss, a friend of Arendt's and Blücher's, gave posthumous voice to their joint presence:

Heinrich with his thin cigars,
his thick Berliner accent, deep down
grumbles, flash-eyed shoutings, spouting
like Vesuvius in their old world living
room amid the clash of amiable minds,

arguing, not less with his friends
and Hannah's, with their dearest intimates,
Homer, Plato, Nietzsche, Kafka, Faulkner,
as though, everlasting in the flesh,
their minds still musing and through him
and her still making up their minds...

The dead poets and philosophers and novelists appear in the living room—both a room for living and a room that lives. They become flesh and blood and can themselves begin to think and judge anew, "still making up their minds." Arendt "argues" with them just as she does with her contemporaries, and simultaneously as though she *were* their contemporary "always within the categories that were available to [them] and that [they] somehow accepted as valid."[44] When Weiss writes that it was as if—through Arendt and Blücher—Homer, Plato, and the others, "everlasting in the flesh" (the "thought made flesh"[45]), were still racking their brains and passing judgment on the times, the living room becomes a stage ("And still they seek the sacred polis" as a later line in the poem has it), a reliable place in which concern for the world is being permanently renegotiated, a place where they can all appear, each one actor and audience in turn. But Arendt goes a step farther. She makes her texts into a stage on which readers, too, are encouraged to free themselves from the power of prevailing opinion and the opinions of the powerful, to disentangle themselves and make their own appearance, liberated from our present's "cords and strings." The world is still being contested and must always be so.[46]

REHEARSING ACTION

In debate with her teacher Karl Jaspers, the communications theorist among the existential philosophers, Hannah Arendt encountered the idea that a text can itself be a performative space where readers are empowered to imagine themselves as agents and even rehearse action, as they do while reading literature. As she wrote in the 1948 essay "What Is Existential Philosophy?,"

> to the extent that Jaspers communicates results, he expresses them in the form of a "playful metaphysics," presenting certain thought processes in a way that is always experimental and never rigidly fixed, having at the same time the character of suggestions that induce others to join with him in thought, to philosophize with him.[47]

In her texts, quotations form a "crisscross network of references"[48] and the many prefixes and prepositions that generate thought and connect worlds undergird trust in the connecting fabric of human affairs. Where in English Arendt often uses elegant passive constructions, in German she chooses active verbs of doing and makes her readers aware of constantly new shades of meaning. Thus she puts onstage the wealth of what mankind has created as well as the plurality of ways of looking at it; writing and reading are shot through with the knowledge that we live in a world constructed by humans, which can therefore also be changed by them.[49]

Characteristic of her writing in German is also the deployment of more powerful rhetorical devices: repetition, alliteration, emphasis, and rhythm. Rhetoric, traditionally regarded skeptically as an attempt to sweep people off their feet, transforms her texts from something legible to something audible. It restores to her language an acoustic dimension that seemed lost in the act of writing it down. Living speech can be answered and contradicted. To hear and be heard, to see and be seen.

In the act of writing, Arendt makes herself audible. She knows that she is speaking into a space and that her texts are always also answers that can be heard. And so the others, the addressees, become, in their turn, answers and animate her to the mobilization of her own imagination. Arendt had come to the conclusion that for Heidegger, thinking always springs back to life behind the thought. Yet according to Arendt, Heidegger's search for the original contexts of words, his thawing out of long-since frozen analogies, is rooted in the arbitrary restriction "that only one person can take a place in the text"[50] — Heidegger himself.

To this closed narrative she opposes one that has been broken open, transforming the method of contemplating alien quotations from reading back to hearing—from "printed results" into "living speech...that can be answered and contradicted."[51] And this is her method whether quoting someone else or writing her own words, thereby urging her readers to want to have a say themselves and giving them the possibility of doing more than just reacting. Through their own associations, readers become her associates. By giving up the authorial narrative point of view, she herself appears in the text as the writer, and by transforming herself from a remote authority (back) into a person making an argument, she creates space—space for other authorizations, for sharing responsibility with readers and helping them to empower themselves. Besides syntax, diction, and sentence structure, Arendt uses rhetorical figures to give her thoughts more voice, that is, to allow the person a more powerful appearance. Her eloquence is not used to persuade. She draws readers not to her side of an argument but rather into the space that she provides, for she "argues" not only with living and dead poets and theoreticians, she argues with the readers as well. In *On Revolution*, her most important text on the yearning for action and the limits of freedom, it is remarkable to what extent Arendt replaces nouns with verbs.[52] People appear before the reader as actors with all their possibilities, room for action, constraints, and (possibly productive) mistakes. In this way, at the same time they read about the opportunities and constraints of historical personages, readers are encouraged to think about their own opportunities, yearnings, and constraints—here reading becomes a rehearsal for action.

> Only great perplexity and real calamity can explain that Jefferson—so conscious of his common sense and so famous for his practical turn of mind—should have proposed these schemes of recurring revolutions.... But the reason Jefferson, throughout his long life, was carried away by such impracticabilities was that he knew, however dimly, that the Revolution, while it had given freedom to the people, had failed to provide a space where this freedom could be exercised.[53]

Near the end of the German version of *On Revolution*, she reminds her readers that

> whoever agrees with Kant that "it is sweet to think up constitutions" will not be able to resist the temptation to continue to

envision this form of government that we are always acquainted with only in *statu nascendi*.[54]

What happens in this passage? Arendt writes a treatise on revolution without presenting a conclusive result of her investigation. She argues with Jefferson as he may have done with himself, and within the categories that were available to him. She transforms the commonly accepted results of history back into something to be negotiated and renegotiated and presents to her readers the political and human dilemmas of the eighteenth century as something worth rethinking. Jefferson becomes our contemporary. Beyond that, she addresses revolutionary wishes and values in her readers: the desire not to sink into lethargy in the face of a political dilemma but to seek new paths to keep the power of revolution "in reserve." Readers transform themselves in thought from consumers to producers. Instead of just consuming the text, they think themselves into it. According to the quote above, the reader can either agree or disagree with Kant, can get involved in things or steer clear of involvement. Readers are empowered to "continue to envision" forms of government. The text speaks to their imaginations. History is freed from its inevitability. With each person who has spoken or acted, who would have spoken or acted, everything could have happened differently. What would happen if the individual, threatened with expendability in mass society, could contradict and be heard? Through the creation of polyphony in the text, other persons become thinkable, persons who enter the living room with other ideas. Readers in the plural really do exist!

———

Hannah Arendt wrote works of political theory whose meaning, thanks to thought images that transcend the reality of the text, is not exhausted even with repeated readings. She manages to do something quite new: readers become (potential) actors in that they achieve self-empowerment. When life is a play within the play carried forward by *amor mundi*, the fear of the judgment of tomorrow loses its crippling power. Freedom—including the great freedom to make mistakes—is born. "We make judgments every hour," said the physicist and aphorist G. C. Lichtenberg, "and we make errors every hour."

Arendt warned of the predominance of social science in which the political would become superfluous. She staged her own texts as a space, as if to put them at the service of endangered politics. Her reflections on the irresolvable contradictions of revolutionary action become a space of sound and speech. Since her sentences are conceived as coming from an actor and not as "objective" descriptions and pronouncements, even exotic, defeated, lost voices and aspects of history can be brought back onto the stage. The stories of defeats are snatched from the jaws of oblivion. Individuals threatened with expendability regain the idea that everything depends on them, on their presence, and that it is their acts or ideas that can "change everything."

———

In the late 1940s, while reading Walter Benjamin, Hermann Broch, and Franz Kafka, Hannah Arendt had noted down that the unity of poetic and speculative content in a work of literature could involve readers in "essential intellectual processes."[55] By means of their own imagination, readers thus activated could set off with the author in search of an "authentic" new idea in the impoverished present. In the strategies of modernism, Arendt said, literature offered readers advice, for it drew them out of the passivity of consumers of novels and made them into active participants in the images with which each author interrogated the world.

In the context of such aesthetic searching, we can today see Arendt's own "performative" writing in a new light. The "dead voices," awaked to new life by Arendt in her desperate assertion "I want to understand," take hold of readers and urge them into thinking co-action, into participation in the joint "performance," the negotiation of the world. Hannah Arendt deprivatized and deindividualized quotidian interpersonal phenomena such as forgiving and promising so that they could find a form appropriate to public appearance, similar to the performance artists searching for new solutions to urgent (and not just artistic) problems of mass society. How can I lure the audience out of its passivity? To reanimate public space in his art, the artist Yves Klein brought the human body down from the canvas and back into the gallery space in his "anthropometries," allowing the audience to imagine that they themselves could also leave an impression on the "canvas" of the world.

Arendt was fond of exaggeration, pushing language beyond the familiar and attempting to jolt thinking out of its habitual ruts and get it back into play through dramatization. In the metaphor of the stage and in her redramatizing of life, traditional notions of the theater no longer held good. The appearance of humans on the stage of the world follows no set script, there are neither divine movers nor the divinely moved. The unlearned metaphor that all the world's a stage now held out the promise that at any moment, anyone through their appearance is capable

of changing "the game," the course of the world. Out of the blue.
Along with the idea of progress, Arendt suspends the idea of the
autonomy of thought. Chance, play, and coincidence come into
their own and the future again becomes what it is: inscrutable,
unexpected, irrational, and illogical. Redemption from the passivity of consumerism and the constraints of society struggles
to recapture public space. By unlearning, by repeatedly tugging
at hobbled interpretation and the threads of her own thought,
Arendt ventured upon "the festival of life."[56]

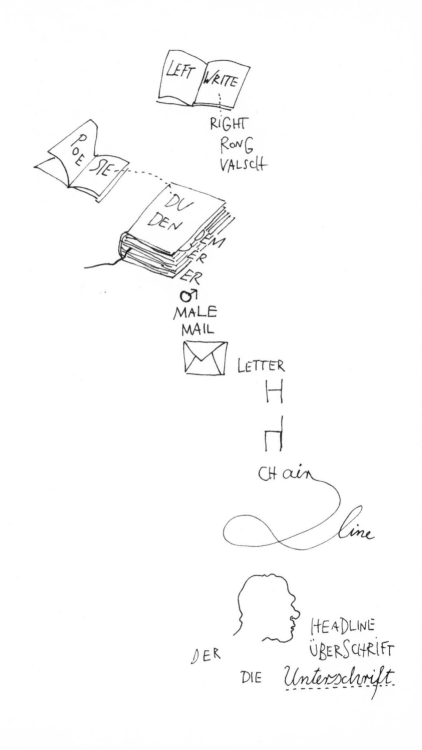

LEFT WRITE

RIGHT
RONG
VALSCH

POE SIE

DU
DEN
DEM
DER
DER
ER

♂ MALE
MAIL

LETTER

CHain

line

HEADLINE
ÜBERSCHRIFT

DER

DIE Unterschrift

APPENDIX: TRANSATLANTIC DIFFERENCES

Translator's Note

For these six side-by-side comparisons of Hannah Arendt's English and German versions of the same passages (five from *The Human Condition/Vita activa* and one from *Men in Dark Times/Menschen in finsteren Zeiten*), I have given first Arendt's English text, then her German text, and then my translation of the latter, in which I try to hew as closely as possible to the order of clauses in Arendt's long sentences. The author's comments on the English and German texts are at the end of each set of texts.

What the public realm considers irrelevant can have such an extraordinary and infectious charm that a whole people may adapt it as their way of life, without for that reason changing its essentially private character. Modern enchantment with "small things," though preached by early twentieth-century poetry in almost all European tongues, has found its classical presentation in the *petit bonheur* of the French people. Since the decay of their once great and glorious public realm, the French have become masters in the art of being happy among "small things," within the space of their own four walls, between chest and bed, table and chair, dog and cat and flowerpot, extending to these things a care and tenderness which, in a world where rapid industrialization constantly kills off the things of yesterday to produce today's objects, may even appear to be the world's last, purely human corner. This enlargement of the private, the enchantment, as it were, of a whole people, does not make it public, does not constitute a public realm, but, on the contrary, means only that the public realm has almost completely receded, so that greatness has given way to charm everywhere; for while the public realm may be great, it cannot be charming precisely because it is unable to harbor the irrelevant.

Dabei kann sogar das, was die Öffentlichkeit für irrelvant ansieht, so faszinierend und bezaubernd reizvoll werden, daß ein ganzes Volk sich ihm zuwendet, in ihm eine Lebensform findet, ohne daß es doch deshalb seinen wesentlich privaten Charakter verlöre. Die moderne Bezauberung von den "kleinen Dingen," wenn sie "dem vereinfachenden Blick der Gewohnheit" sich entziehen, "jenes rätselhafte, wortlose, schrankenlose Entzücken", das aufbricht vor dem "von niemand beachteten Daliegen oder—lehnen"—"einer Gießkanne, einer auf dem Felde verlassenen Egge, einem Hund in der Sonne, einem ärmlichen Kirchhof, einem Krüppel, einem kleinen Bauernhaus"—, daß alles dies "Gefäß einer Offenbarung" werden kann (*footnote*: Ich verwende hier Bilder aus Lord Chandos, ich hätte ebenso gut auch George oder Rilke zitieren können.), wissen wir, wenn schon nicht von uns selbst, so aus der europäischen Dichtung des frühen zwanzigsten Jahrhunderts; aber seine klassische Verwirklichung als eine Lebensform hat dies Entzücken wohl nur in dem gefunden, was man in Frankreich "le petit bonheur" nennt. Die eigentümlich bezaubernde Zärtlichkeit des französischen Alltags, der ineins zart und handfest-volkstümlich ist, entstand, als die einst große und ruhmreiche Öffentlichkeit der Nation zerfiel und der Verfall das Volk in das Private drängte, wo es sich dann als Meister erwies in der Kunst glücklich zu sein in den eigenen vier Wänden, zwischen Bett und Schrank, Tisch und Stuhl, umgeben von Hund, Katze und Blumentopf. Die zärtliche Sorgfalt und Vorsorge, die in diesem engsten Bereich waltet, mag wohl in einer Welt, deren rapide Industrialisierung ständig die Dinge des gewohnten Gestern zerstört, um Platz zu schaffen für die Erzeugung des

Neuen, anmuten, als habe sich hierhin die letzte, rein menschliche Freude an der Welt geflüchtet. Aber diese Ausweitung des Privaten, dieser Zauber, den gleichsam ein ganzes Volk über den Alltag gebreitet hat, stellt keinen öffentlichen Raum bereit, sondern bedeutet im Gegenteil nur, daß das Öffentliche aus dem Leben des Volkes nahezu vollständig geschwunden ist, so daß überall das Entzücken und der Zauber, und nicht Größe oder Bedeutung, vorwalten. Denn bezaubernd gerade kann das Öffentliche, das sich der Größe eignet, niemals sein, und zwar eben darum, weil es für das Irrelevante keinen Platz hat.

[Yet even what the public realm considers irrelevant can become so fascinating and enchantingly lovely that a whole people turns to it, finding in it a way of life, yet it still retains its essentially private character. The modern enchantment with "small things" when they elude "the simplifying eyes of habit," "that mysterious, wordless, limitless delight" that erupts when we see lying or leaning somewhere a "watering can, a harrow left in the field, a dog in the sun, a poor churchyard, a cripple, the little cottage of a farmer" — we know that all this can become the "vessel of a revelation" (footnote: I quote here images from Hugo von Hofmannsthal's "Letter of Lord Chandos." I could just as well have quoted Stefan George or Rilke.), if not from our own experience, then from European poetry of the early twentieth century; but this delight has found its classic realization as a way of life only in what the French call "le petit bonheur." The curiously enchanting tenderness of everyday life in France, which is at the same time gentle and stoutly of the people, arose when the once great and glorious public realm of the nation declined and that decay drove people into private life, where they then proved themselves masters in the art of being happy within their own four walls, between bed and chest, table and chair, *surrounded by dog, cat, and flowerpot. The tender care and solicitude that prevail in this most restricted realm may well, in a world whose rapid industrialization constantly destroys the familiar yesterday to clear the way for the production of new things, make it seem that the last purely human enjoyment of the world had found refuge here. This enlargement of the private, however, this magic that an entire people seems to spread over everyday life, does not provide a public space but on the contrary means only that what is public has almost completely disappeared from the life of the people, so that everywhere charm and enchantment prevail but not greatness or significance. For while what is public may be great, it cannot be charming, precisely because it is unable to harbor the irrelevant.]*

I. COMMENTS

The English passage on the threat to public space and the cult of private life at the beginning of the twentieth century clearly makes a more terse impression. It has a spare elegance compared to the German version, during whose composition Arendt probably was recalling Benjamin's "destructive character" (*Platz schaffen* — "clear the way") and Broch's study of Hofmannsthal, which she was rereading because she was also getting her essay on Broch ready for publication. It seems that Arendt added to the German version what had already been in the back of her mind while writing the English version — images from German literature of the interwar period (Hofmannsthal) that conjured up the "small things" in all their private character. As she noted in her footnote, she could just as well have quoted from Rilke or Stefan George.

In other ways, too, the German version is more strongly developed (*das gewohnte Gestern* — "the familiar yesterday," *die rein menschliche Freude an der Welt* — "the purely human enjoyment of the world," *seine klassische Verwirklichung als eine Lebensform* — "its classic realization as a way of life"), whereas the English version plays with the gap between "yesterday" and "today." While the concept of "the public realm" is simply repeated in English, the German version distinguishes between *die Öffentlichkeit* — "the public realm," *ein öffentlicher Raum* — "a public space," *das Öffentliche* — "what is public," and *die Öffentlichkeit der Nation* — "the public realm of the nation," whereby the idea of the *grande nation* is also evoked in the imagination of the reader.

Where in English Arendt often chooses elegant but fairly static verbs, in German she uses powerfully active verbs (*Platz schaffen*—"clear the way," *stellt...bereit*—"provides," *in das Private drängte*—"drove...into private life"), as if to let her language exude the longing or perhaps the assurance that we live in a world built by men and thus also amenable to change by men.

By stretching out a thought over two different yet related and sometimes similar-sounding words, as in the rhetorical device of hendiadys (*zerfiel und der Verfall*—"declined and that decay," *faszinierend und bezaubernd reizvoll*—"fascinating and enchantingly lovely," *große und ruhmreiche*—"great and glorious," *Sorgfalt und Vorsorge*—"care and solicitude"), she stages the text as a space. Where sentences do not run straight ahead like one-way streets, where the flow of thought gets interrupted and set in relation to other possibilities, the reader too can get caught up in its movement.

However, neither the enormous increase in fertility nor the socialization of the process, that is, the substitution of society or collective mankind for individual men as its subject, can eliminate the character of strict and even cruel privacy from the experience of bodily processes in which life manifests itself, or from the activity of laboring itself.

Nun kann aber offenbar weder die ungeheuer gesteigerte Produktivität bzw. Fruchtbarkeit des Arbeits- und Lebensprozesses noch seine eventuelle Vergesellschaftung verhindern, daß die ihnen entsprechenden Erfahrungen privatester Natur bleiben und sich der Mitteilbarkeit ebenso entziehen wie alle sonstigen körperlichen Erfahrungen; zwischen der Mühsal der Arbeit, für die das körperlich Lebendigsein zur Last und Bürde des Menschseins wird, und den "heillosen Schmerzen im leiblichen Geweb" bestehen nur Gradunterschiede der Intensität, denn ihre "Höllischkeit" — die Arbeitshölle oder die Schmerzenshölle — liegt gerade darin, daß sie, was den Menschen als ein weltliches Wesen anlangt, "nicht von hier" sind — "ein Grimm der Hölle, nicht von hier" (Rilke). Sie sind unmitteilbar und unaussprechlich, weil die Sprache, was immer unsere Theorien darüber sein mögen, hartnäckig darauf besteht, sich an der Welt und ihrer dinglichen Gegenständlichkeit zu orientieren, und dies in einem solchen Maße, daß für das absolut Private und Subjektive selbst ihre metaphorische Kraft versagt.

[Obviously, however, neither the enormously increased productivity (or fertility) of the process of work and life nor its eventual socialization can prevent the nature of the experiences that correspond to them from remaining extremely private and resisting communication, just as all other bodily experiences do; the differences between the drudgery of work, for which physical existence becomes the onus and burden of being human, and the "unholy pains in the fabric of the body" are only ones of degree of intensity, for their "hellishness" — the hell of work or the hell of pain — consists precisely in the fact that, to the extent that

man is a worldly being, they are "not from here" (Rilke).[1] They are unmediated and inexpressible, because language, whatever our theories about it may be, stubbornly insists on orienting itself to the world and its material concreteness to such a degree that even its metaphorical power fails for what is absolutely private and subjective.]

II. COMMENTS

Again, the German version is strongly rhetorical, with powerful images and verbs. From behind the "cruel privacy" of the English emerges the "hellishness" of Rilke's pain in the German, which was probably already in the back of Arendt's mind as she was writing the English. Since speech orients itself to "the world and its material concreteness," it is no wonder that it is different in different cultures.

For translators of Arendt's *The Human Condition* into other languages, a comparison of the German version of such a passage would be extremely helpful, if not imperative. That "cruel" here must not be understood as "mean" or "sadistic" would be immediately obvious from a look at the version in Arendt's native language, which actually should be the basis of any translation.

III. *THE HUMAN CONDITION*, P. 9

The human condition comprehends more than the conditions under which life has been given to man. Men are conditioned beings because everything they come in contact with turns immediately into a condition of their existence. The world in which the vita activa spends itself consists of things produced by human activities; but the things that owe their existence exclusively to men nevertheless constantly condition their human makers.

Nun umfaßt aber die Condition humaine, die menschliche Bedingtheit im Ganzen, mehr als nur die Bedingungen, unter denen den Menschen das Leben auf der Erde gegeben ist. Menschen sind bedingte Wesen, weil ein jegliches, womit sie in Berührung kommen, sich unmittelbar in eine Bedingung ihrer Existenz verwandelt. Die Welt, in der die Vita activa sich bewegt, besteht im wesentlichen aus Dingen, die Gebilde von Menschenhand sind; und diese Dinge, die ohne den Menschen nie entstanden wären, sind wiederum Bedingung menschlicher Existenz.

[Now the condition humaine, human conditionality in general, comprises more than just the conditions under which life on earth is given to men. Human beings are conditioned beings because everything they come into contact with is immediately transformed into a condition of their existence. The world in which the vita activa moves consists essentially of things that are the works of men's hands; and these things, which never would have come into being without man, are in their turn the conditions of human existence.]

III. COMMENTS

Prefixes and prepositions in their restricted number sustain and carry Arendt's language. They marshal the nouns and establish relationships between them. While in English the idea of this passage is woven from the prefix "con-" (*condition, contact, consists, constantly*), German works with the prefix "be-" (*Bedingtheit*—"conditionality," *Bedingungen*—"conditions," *Berührung*—"contact," *sich bewegt*—"moves," *besteht*—"consists"). Theodor Fontane's "*Gebilde von Menschenhand*"—"works of men's hands" (which we have already encountered in "Introduction *into* Politics," see page 103 above) stands in place of "things produced by human activities" in the English version. In a later passage, the knowledge of the transience of the world that resonates from Fontane's complete sentence (*Tand, Tand / Ist das Gebilde von Menschenhand*—"Baubles, baubles / Are the works of men's hands") is rendered in English as "human artifices."

Without being forgiven, released from the consequences of what
we have done, our capacity to act would, as it were, be confined
to one single deed from which we could never recover; we would
remain the victims of its consequences forever, not unlike the
sorcerer's apprentice who lacked the formula to break the spell.
Without being bound to the fulfillment of promises, we would
never be able to keep our identities; we would be condemned to
wander helplessly and without direction in the darkness of each
man's lonely heart, caught in its contradictions and equivocali-
ties—a darkness which only the light shed over the public realm
through the presence of others, who confirm the identity between
the one who promises and the one who fulfills, can dispel.

IV. *VITA ACTIVA*, P. 302
(SECOND PARAGRAPH NOT IN ENGLISH VERSION)

Könnten wir einander nicht vergeben, d.h. uns gegenseitig von
den Folgen unserer Taten wieder entbinden, so beschränkte sich
unsere Fähigkeit zu handeln gewissermaßen auf eine einzige Tat,
deren Folgen uns bis an unser Lebensende im wahrsten Sinne
des Wortes verfolgen würde, im Guten wie im Bösen; gerade im
Handeln wären wir das Opfer unserer selbst, als seien wir der Zau-
berlehrling, der das erlösende Wort Besen, Besen, sei's gewesen,
nicht findet. Ohne uns durch Versprechen für eine ungewisse
Zukunft zu binden und auf sie einzurichten, wären wir niemals
imstande, die eigene Identität durchzuhalten; wir wären hilflos
der Dunkelheit des menschlichen Herzens, seinen Zweideutig-
keiten und Widersprüchen ausgeliefert, verirrt in einem Labyrinth einsamer Stimmungen, aus dem wir nur erlöst werden
können durch den Ruf der Mitwelt, die dadurch, daß sie uns auf
die Versprechen festlegt, die wir gegeben haben und nun halten
sollen, in unserer Identitat bestätigt, bzw. diese Identität überhaupt erst konstitutiert.

…Die Fähigkeiten, zu verzeihen und zu versprechen, sind in
dem Vermögen des Handelns verwurzelt; sie sind die Modi, durch
die der Handelnde von einer Vergangenheit, die ihn auf immer
festlegen will, befreit wird, und sich in einer Zukunft, deren
Unabsehbarkeit bedroht, halbwegs versichern kann.

[If we were not able to forgive each other, i.e., to release each other from
the consequences of our acts, our ability to act would to a certain extent
be restricted to one single deed, whose consequences would, in the most
literal sense of the word, pursue us to the end of our lives for better or

for worse; precisely in action we would be our own victim, as if we were the sorcerer's apprentice who cannot find the magic formula, "Broom, broom, leave the room." Without committing ourselves to and preparing for an uncertain future through the act of promising, we would never be able to keep hold of our own identity; we would be helplessly at the mercy of the darkness of the human heart, its ambiguities and contradictions, lost in the labyrinth of lonely moods from which we can be redeemed only through the call of our fellow men who, by holding us to the promises we have made and now must keep, confirm us in our identity, or rather, constitute that identity in the first place.

. . . The capacities to forgive and to promise both have their roots in our ability to act; they are the modes through which the agent is freed from a past that always wants to determine him, and through which he can halfway ensure himself a future whose unpredictability is threatening.]

IV. COMMENTS

Whereas in English, the thought is developed through the two structures introduced by "without" ("Without being forgiven...," "Without being bound..."), in German it is the powerful subjunctive verbs that hold the sentence together (*Könnten wir... nicht*—"If we were not able to," *beschränkte sich*—"would...be restricted," *wären wir*—"we would be," etc.) and thereby articulate even more forcefully the wish—better, the yearning—for the existence of such a forgiveness as the guarantor of freedom. The *Ruf der Mitwelt*—"the call of our fellow men"—brings an end to the subjunctive constructions. The replacement of subjunctive with the indicative (*erlöst werden können*—"can...be redeemed," *uns... festlegt*—"holds us," etc.) signals responsibility for the actions. In this passage, the cohesion of the world is guaranteed by the repetition of the prefix *Ver-*, which can tell us that *Verbrechen* (crime), *Versprechen* (promise), and *Verzeihen* (forgiving) coexist in the world.

Everything indicated that the poet had found a new voice—perhaps "the dying swan's song that is held to be the most beautiful"—but when the moment came for the voice to be heard, it seemed to have lost its power. This is the only objective and therefore unquestionable sign we have that he had transgressed the rather wide limits set for poets, that he had crossed the line marking what was permitted to him. For these boundaries, alas, cannot be detected from the outside, and can hardly even be guessed at. They are like faint ridges, all but invisible to the naked eye, which, once a man has crossed them—or not even actually crossed them but just stumbled over them—suddenly grow into walls. There is no retracing of steps; whatever he does, he finds himself with his back against the wall. And even now, *après coup*, it is difficult to define the cause; our only evidence that the step was taken is supplied by the poetry, and all it tells us is the moment when it happened, when the punishment caught up with him. For the only punishment that a poet can suffer, short of death, is, of course, the sudden loss of what throughout human history has appeared a divine gift.

Das ist wenig, doch gerade gut genug, um zu zeigen, daß der
alternde Dichter eine neue Stimme gefunden hatte—vielleicht
die des "sterbenden Schwans," dessen Gesang als der schön-
ste gilt. Aber als der Augenblick kam, diese Stimme ertönen
zu lassen, scheint sie ihre Kraft verloren zu haben. Und dies
ist der einzige handgreifliche, unbezweifelbare Beweis dafur,
daß Brecht die weiten, auch dem Dichter gesetzten Grenzen
des Erlaubten überschritten, beziehungsweise die gerade ihm
gesetzte Grenze verletzt hatte. Innerhalb der Dichtung läßt sich
die Grenzüberschreitung nachweisen, aber von außen läßt sich
nicht sagen, worin sie nun eigentlich besteht. Denn diese Grenzen sind durch keine Verhaltensregeln markert oder markerbar;
sie sind wie flüchtige, dem Auge kaum sichtbare Linien, die erst,
wenn sie überschritten sind und man sie hinter sich gelassen hat,
unvermutet zu Mauern emporwachsen. Nun kann man plötzlich
nicht mehr zurück, man steht mit dem Rücken gegen die Wand
und mag selbst jetzt noch nicht wissen, wie es alles gekommen
ist—als habe man die Grenze gar nicht wirklich überschritten,
sondern sei nur gleichsam irgendwie über sie gestolpert. Das
einzige, was nicht zu bestreiten ist, ist das Aussetzen der Begabung, nicht jeglicher Begabung, aber eben der höchsten. Man
kann die Dichter nicht bestrafen (wenn man sie ins Gefängnis
setzt, hören sie darum noch lange nicht auf zu dichten), weil die
einzige Strafe, die sie erleiden können, sofern man sie nur überhaupt am Leben läßt, der plötzliche Verlust dessen ist, was seit eh
und je als eine Gabe der Götter gegolten hat.

[*It's not much, but it's just good enough to show that the aging poet had found a new voice—perhaps that of the "dying swan" whose song is supposed to be the most beautiful. But when the moment came to let this voice heard, it seems to have lost its power. And this is the only palpable, unquestionable proof that Brecht had overstepped the wide limits, which apply even to poets, of what is permitted, or rather, he had transgressed the limits that applied to him alone. From within poetry, one can identify the transgression of limits, but from outside poetry, one cannot say what the transgression actually consists of. For these limits neither are, nor can be, indicated by any code of behavior; they are like transient lines, almost imperceptible to the naked eye, and only when they have been overstepped and left behind do they unexpectedly rise up as walls. Now suddenly there is no turning back. One stands with one's back to the wall and may not yet even know oneself how it happened—as if one had not really overstepped the boundary, but only somehow stumbled over it. The only thing that is incontestable is the failure of one's gift, not every gift, only the highest one. Poets cannot be punished (even if you put them in jail they keep writing), because the only punishment they can suffer, to the extent that they're allowed to continue living at all, is the sudden loss of what has always been considered a gift of the gods.*]

V. COMMENTS

In this passage from Arendt's 1967 essay on Brecht, we can see various ways she goes about what Randall Jarrell described as combining "English instantness with German philosophical discipline."[2] At the beginning of the German version, we hear an echo of Brecht's line *Dies ist nun alles und ist nicht genug* — "This then is everything and not enough."[3] Where in English Arendt alludes to the proverb "What is permitted to Jove," in German she speaks more dryly of "the limits that even apply to poets." The English passage persists for a long time within the concrete image, while the German leaves room for more reflective language.

The blessing of life as a whole, inherent in labor, can never be found in work and should not be mistaken for the inevitably brief spell of relief and joy which follows accomplishment and attends achievement. The blessing of labor is that effort and gratification follow each other as closely as producing and consuming the means of subsistence, so that happiness is a concomitant of the process itself, just as pleasure is a concomitant of the functioning of a healthy body. The "happiness of the greatest number," into which we have generalized and vulgarized the felicity with which earthly life has always been blessed, conceptualized into an "ideal" the fundamental reality of a laboring humanity. The right to the pursuit of this happiness is indeed as undeniable as the right to life; it is even identical with it. But it has nothing in common with good fortune, which is rare and never lasts and cannot be pursued, because fortune depends on luck and what chance gives and takes, although most people in their "pursuit of happiness" run after good fortune and make themselves unhappy even when it befalls them, because they want to keep and enjoy luck as though it were an inexhaustible abundance of "good things."

VI. *VITA ACTIVA*, PP. 126–127

Diesen Segen, den das Arbeiten über ein ganzes Leben breiten
kann, kann das Herstellen niemals leisten, denn es handelt sich
hier keineswegs um die immer kurzen Augenblicke der Erleich-
terung und Freude, die sich einstellen, wenn eine Leistung vollen-
det ist. Der Segen der Arbeit ist, daß Mühsal und Lohn einander in
dem gleichen regelmäßigen Rhythmus folgen wie Arbeiten und
Essen, die Zubereitung der Lebensmittel und ihr Verzehr, so daß
ein Lustgefühl den gesamten Vorgang begleitet, nicht anders als
das Funktionieren eines gesunden Körpers. Diese Lust, mit der das
irdische Leben immer gesegnet war, hat die Neuzeit in das "Glück
der größten Anzahl" verallgemeinert und vulgarisiert, aber sie
hat damit nur zu einem Ideal erhoben, was die selbstverständli-
che Wirklichkeit des arbeitenden Menschen ist. Das Recht, nach
diesem Glück zu trachten, ist so unbestreitbar wie das Recht auf
Leben, es ist sogar mit ihm identisch. Nur haben Lust wie Segen
mit Glück im eigentlichen Sinne nichts zu tun. Denn das Glück,
das Fortuna spendet, ist selten und immer flüchtig und kann
nicht verfolgt werden; es hängt am Zufall, an dem, was Goethe
die "Gelegenheit" nannte, die gibt und nimmt, und die "Jagd
nach diesem Glück" endet auch dann im Unglück, wenn Fortuna
sich zufällig zeigen sollte, weil die Jagenden die Lust meinen, und
nicht das Glück, und es also behalten und genießen wollen, als
handele es sich um ein unerschöpfliches Füllhorn der Natur.

[*This blessing, which labor can spread over an entire life, can never be
provided by production, for we are not talking about the always short
moments of relief and joy that arise when a job is completed. The blessing
of labor is that effort and reward follow each other in the same regular*

rhythm as working and eating, the preparation of ingredients and their consumption, so that a feeling of pleasure accompanies the entire process, no different from the functioning of a healthy body. This pleasure, with which earthly life has always been blessed, has in modern times been generalized and vulgarized as the "happiness of the greater number," thereby simply elevating to an ideal the fundamental reality of working humanity. The right to pursue this happiness is as uncontested as the right to life. In fact they are identical. Pleasure, however, like a blessing, has nothing to do with good fortune in its fundamental meaning. For the happiness that good fortune brings is rare and always fleeting and cannot be pursued; it depends on chance, on what Goethe called the "Gelegenheit" (opportunity) that gives and takes away, and the "hunt for this happiness" ends in unhappiness even when good fortune happens to show itself, because the hunters of happiness are pursuing pleasure and not good fortune, and thus want to hold on to and enjoy it as if it were an inexhaustible cornucopia of nature.]

VI. COMMENTS

An example of textual cross feed that goes down two different paths in the two languages. In the English original, the passage centers on the "pursuit of happiness" of the American Declaration of Independence. Arendt clearly differentiates this notion from Jeremy Bentham's utilitarian one of "the happiness of the greater number," which dominated contemporary American social science. The extremely rhythmical German version, by contrast, is oriented to the "hunt for happiness" and follows a different set of terminological roots. Along with the idea of *Lust*—"pleasure," it brings into the text Goethe's attack on poetasters:

> *Willst du dich als Dichter beweisen*
> *So mußt du nicht Helden noch Hirten preisen,*
> *Hier ist Rhodus! Tanze du Wicht*
> *Und der Gelegenheit schaff' ein Gedicht!*

> If you want to prove yourself a poet
> There's no need to praise heroes and shepherds.
> Here is Rhodes! Dance, you poor wight,
> And from opportunity make a poem!

We can only speculate about whether Arendt also had Brecht's *"Das Lied von der Unzulänglichkeit menschlichen Strebens"* (Song of the Inadequacy of Human Ambition) from *The Threepenny Opera* in the back of her mind:

> *Ja, renn nur nach dem Glück*
> *Doch renne nicht zu sehr!*
> *Denn alle rennen nach dem Glück*
> *Das Glück rennt hinterher.*

Denn für dieses Leben
Ist der Mensch nicht anspruchslos genug
Drum ist all sein Streben
Nur ein Selbstbetrug.

Go and run after happiness
But don't run too hard!
For everyone runs after happiness
And happiness brings up the rear.

>Because for this life
>Man isn't undemanding enough
>That's why in all his striving
>He's just fooling himself.

NOTES

PREFACE

1. This is the last strophe of the poem "Die öffentlichen Verleumder" (The public slanderers) by the Swiss poet and novelist Gottfried Keller (1819–1890). The text was widely circulated among opponents of the Nazis and is quoted by Thomas Mann in an essay he wrote after the German invasion of Poland in 1939.–Trans.

2. An English translation can be found in Ingeborg Bachmann, *Three Paths to the Lake* (Teaneck, NJ: Holmes and Meier, 1997).–Trans.

3. Among other places, she quoted Keller's poem in a letter to Martin Heidegger of May 6, 1950.

4. http://gutenberg.spiegel.de/buch/2981/112; also in Walter Benjamin, *Gesammelte Schriften III: Kritiken und Rezensionen 1912–1931* (Frankfurt: Suhrkamp, 1991).

5. See the section on Heinrich Heine in Arendt's 1944 essay "The Jew as Pariah: A Hidden Tradition," in The *Jew as Pariah*, 69–75.

6. *The Human Condition*, 176.

7. *Zur Zeit*.

8. In a 1964 West German television interview with Günter Gaus, English translation, "'What Remains? The Language Remains': A Conversation with Günter Gaus," in *Essays in Understanding*, 11.

9. Hahn, *Hannah Arendt*, 20.

10. See the catalog that accompanied the exhibition: Hahn and Knott, *Hannah Arendt — Von den Dichtern erwarten wir Wahrheit*. The

documents from Schocken Books influenced my chapter on translation; the correspondence with Dolf Sternberger and Charlotte Beradt, the chapter on laughter; the correspondence with W. H. Auden, the chapter on forgiveness; and the long poem "A Living Room," the chapter on dramatization.

LAUGHTER

1. From the 1933 poem "Deutschland." This is also the epigraph Hannah Arendt chose for *Eichmann in Jerusalem*. —Trans.

2. Elon, "Excommunication of Hannah Arendt," vii.

3. *Eichmann in Jerusalem*, 26.

4. Ibid.

5. *Ich will verstehen*, 41.

6. *Eichmann in Jerusalem*, foreword to the German edition, 15–16.

7. Arendt uses "thoughtlessness" throughout *Eichmann in Jerusalem* as the equivalent of German *Gedankenlosigkeit*, which carries more strongly the connotation of "absence of thought" rather than "lack of consideration for others."—Trans.

8. *Eichmann in Jerusalem*, 11.

9. Ibid., 12.

10. Ibid., 125.

11. Arendt/Scholem, *Briefwechsel*, 432.

12. Letter from Karl Jaspers to Hannah Arendt, November 16, 1963, Arendt/Jaspers, *Correspondence*, 531.

13. In her responses to questions posed by a symposium in the *Jewish World* in September 1964, Arendt addressed in detail the desperate situation of the Jewish councils: "Objectively speaking, there were hardly more than three alternatives: to admit their impotence and to tell the people all is lost, *sauve qui peut*; or to accompany their charges on the

voyage to the East and suffer the same fate; or, as was notably done in France, to use the Nazi-controlled Jewish council as a cover for underground work in which one tried to help Jews to escape." *The Jewish Writings*, 494.

14. Letter from Hannah Arendt to Klaus Piper, Deutsches Literaturarchiv, Marbach.

15. *The Jewish Writings*, 494.

16. Partially available in German at www.hannaharendt.de/download/fest_interview.pdf. An English translation is in preparation from Melville House, Brooklyn, New York.

17. From a 1964 interview with Thilo Koch, in which Arendt said, "The idea that evil is demonic, which...sees its precedence in the tale of the fallen angel Lucifer, is extraordinarily appealing to people.... Precisely because these criminals were not driven by the evil and murderous motives that we're familiar with—they murdered not to murder, but simply as part of their career—it seemed only too obvious to us all that we needed to demonize the catastrophe in order to find some historical meaning in it." *The Jewish Writings*, 487–88.

18. *Eichmann in Jerusalem*, 80.

19. Arendt/Scholem, *Briefwechsel*, 433. An English translation is in preparation from the University of Chicago Press.

20. *The Jewish Writings*, 468.

21. *Essays in Understanding*, 16. In his interesting essay "Das Lachen der Hannah Arendt" (Hannah Arendt's Laughter), Thomas Wild characterizes her laughter as an "expression of judgment." Laughter is "not an expression of superiority or disparagement nor a physical release. Arendt's laughter is the laughter of spontaneity." In *Dichterisch Denken*, ed. Heuer and von der Lühe (Göttingen: Wallstein Verlag, 2007), 116.

22. *Eichmann in Jerusalem*, 252.

23. *The Jewish Writings*, 169.

24. Benjamin, "Der Autor als Produzent," *Gesammelte Schriften* II/2, 699.

25. *Essays in Understanding*, 73–74. See also Marie Luise Knott, "Hannah Arendt liest Franz Kafka 1944," *Text und Kritik* 166/167 (2005): 150–61.

26. *Essays in Understanding*, 78.

27. *The Jewish Writings*, 269.

28. Ibid., 264–65.

29. All quotes are from the manuscript's foreword and its planned chapter on laughter in *Hannah-Buch*, Kapitel VII, Nachlass Karl Jaspers, Deutsches Literaturarchiv, Marbach am Neckar.

30. "Gedenkrede auf Karl Jaspers" (March 4, 1969), in Arendt/Jaspers, *Briefwechsel*, 719.

31. Stefan George (1868–1933) was a modernist poet who gathered around himself a cult following of young men, including Claus von Stauffenberg and his two brothers. Another of George's disciples was the Jewish historian Ernst Kantorowicz (1895–1963), who fled Nazi Germany and later taught at Berkeley and Princeton.—Trans.

32. After visiting Jaspers in 1952, she wrote to her husband, Heinrich Blücher, "For Jaspers it is ultimately tradition that is valid and sets standards.... Among the moderns he *de facto* acknowledges only those who are epigones. The day I arrived Jaspers' rationalizing and moralizing had increased so much that I was almost at my wit's end. But then I brought him round again, because he *is* such a marvelous fellow, there's no one like him." *Within Four Walls*, 154.

33. From Willem Sassen's interview with Eichmann in Argentina as quoted in the docudrama *Eichmanns Ende*. Sassen was a Dutch Nazi. Parts of the interview, transcribed and edited by Sassen, first appeared in English in *Life* magazine, November 28 and December 5, 1960.

34. Both quotes are from the rubric "Ironie," in *Historisches Wörter-buch der Philosophie*, Vol. 4, 577, 579.

35. J. Glenn Gray to Hannah Arendt, March 23, 1963, Library of Congress, Arendt Papers, Box 11.

36. *The Origins of Totalitarianism*, 459.

37. Ibid., 443.

38. *The Jewish Writings*, 488. Instead of the bland and misleading translation "average man on the street," the original German of this 1964 interview with Thilo Koch has "*beliebiger Hanswurst*" (random buffoon). Cf. *Ich will verstehen*, 41.

39. Baumgart, "Mit Mördern leben," 483.

40. *Witz* in German and *wit* in English are both derived from roots meaning "to know" (*wissen* in German).—Trans.

41. Immanuel Kant, *Anthropologie in pragmatischer Hinsicht* (Hamburg: Felix Meiner, 2000), § 54.

42. "Un salto ecuestre que de la imaginación."

43. Hannah Arendt to Benno von Wiese, February 19, 1965, in Rossade, "'Dem Zeitgeist erlegen,'" 183. Von Wiese (1903–1987) was a friend from Arendt's student days in Heidelberg who also studied with Karl Jaspers. He joined the National Socialist party in 1933 and was an apologist for the regime during the Third Reich. After the war he became a professor of literature at the University of Bonn.—Trans.

44. *Essays in Understanding*, 11, with interpolations by the author in brackets.

45. An English translation is available in Gunther Neske and Emil Kettering, eds., *Martin Heidegger and National Socialism* (New York: Paragon House, 1990), 5–13.—Trans.

46. Plessner, *Das Lachen und das Weinen*, 377.

47. *The Jew as Pariah*, 250–51, and Arendt/Scholem, *Briefwechsel*, 444.

The passage in square brackets is not in the German edition and the passage in curly brackets is not in the English edition.

48. "Nathalie Sarraute," 6.

49. Ibid., 6, 5.

50. See note 33 above.

51. *Eichmann in Jerusalem*, 252.

52. *Partisan Review*, March 1964, 91. Also in *Between Friends*, 167n6.

53. All quotes are from Arendt's letter to McCarthy, June 23, 1964, *Between Friends*, 168.

54. *Essays in Understanding*, 128.

55. *Responsibility and Judgment*, 150.

56. *The Life of the Mind*, 1:3.

57. Ibid., 1:4.

58. Ibid., 1:5.

TRANSLATION

1. "A Guide for Youth: Martin Buber," in *The Jewish Writings*, 31–33.

2. Ibid., 32. In Arendt's original French, "cette voie singulièrement détournée."

3. See Lambert Schneider, ed., *Rechenschaft über vierzig Jahre Verlagsarbeit, 1925–1965: Ein Almanach* (Heidelberg: Schneider, 1965), 12.

4. *Essays in Understanding*, 318.

5. Ibid., 309–10.

6. *Men in Dark Times*, 170.

7. Joachim Fest, "Das Mädchen aus der Fremde," in *Der Spiegel*, September 13, 2004, 142–46, www.spiegel.de/spiegel/print/d-32134693.html.

8. *The Jewish Writings*, 300.

9. *Within Four Walls*, 209 (letter of July 25, 1952).

10. Gaus interview in *Ich will verstehen*, 61; entire interview available in German at www.youtube.com/watch?v=tWZqS2uYvbY.

11. Améry, "Das Leben zwischen den Sprachen," 37.

12. Karl Jaspers wrote in 1947 that forgetting the metaphoric character of language prepared the ground for a false sense of authenticity. *Von der Wahrheit*, 398.

13. *Denktagebuch*, 728.

14. Herta Müller, *Züricher Poetik Dozentur*, November 19, 2007.

15. *Men in Dark Times*, 264. Conversely, for Jarrell, German was a country made of sounds. "I believe my favorite country's German" he wrote in his poem "Deutsch Durch Freud" (German through Freud): "It is by Trust, and Love, and reading Rilke / Without *ein Wörterbuch*, that man learns German."

16. Arendt/Heidegger, *Letters*, 60.

17. "Das Mädchen aus der Fremde" is the poem Friedrich Schiller used as the epigraph to each of his poetry collections. The girl from abroad "...brought them fruits and flowers, / ripened on other meadows, / in another sunlight / and a more fortunate nature, / and gave to each a gift, / fruits to one and flowers to another. / The youth and the old man on his cane / each went home with a present." Schiller, *Sämtliche Werke*, 1: 408.—Trans.

18. Hermann Broch, "Einige Bemerkungen zur Philosophie und Technik des Übersetzens," in *Dichten und Erkennen*, ed. Hannah Arendt (Zurich: Rhein Verlag, 1955), 277ff; Walter Benjamin, "The Task of the Translator: An Introduction to the Translation of Baudelaire's *Tableaux Parisiens*," in *Illuminations*, 69–82; Franz Rosenzweig, "Nachwort zu den Hymnen und Gedichten des Jehuda Halevi," 200–19.

19. Rosenzweig, "Nachwort zu den Hymnen und Gedichten des Jehuda Halevi," 202.

20. Benjamin, *Illuminations*, 72, 80–81.

21. On quotations in montage, see Heuer, *Arendt-Handbuch*, 162–86; on the significance of literature for Arendt, see the analyses in Hahn, *Hannah Arendt*.

22. Letter from Hannah Arendt to J. Glenn Gray, December 11, 1967, Library of Congress, Hannah Arendt Papers, Box 11.

23. "If thou wouldst give thy heart to me, do it secretly," a text by an unknown poet, set to music by Johann Sebastian Bach under the title "Aria di Giovannini" (BWV 518).—Trans.

24. Arendt and McCarthy, *Between Friends*, 224 (letter of December 16, 1968).

25. Heuer, Heiter, and Rosenmüller, *Arendt-Handbuch*, 13; see especially the entry on Arendt's bilingual writings.

26. Quoted in Hahn and Knott, *Hannah Arendt*, 188.

27. Arendt/Scholem, *Briefwechsel*, 345.

28. Brauer, *The Problem with Reading Hannah Arendt in English*, 3.

29. *Denktagebuch*, 772.

30. Randall Jarrell, *Randall Jarrell's Letters: An Autobiographical and Literary Selection*, ed. Mary Jarrell (Charlottesville: University of Virginia Press, 2002), 245.

31. Auden, "Thinking What We Are Doing," 72.

32. Walter Benjamin, "Zum gesellschaftlichen Standort des französischen Schriftstellers," *Gesammelte Schriften* II/2, 776–803.

33. The illuminating distinction between "vision" and "version" was the invention of the bilingual author and translator Esther Kinsky at the 2008 conference "'Happy bin ich schon, aber glücklich bin ich nicht': Autoren übersetzen sich selbst" ("I'm happy, but I'm not glücklich": Authors Translating Themselves) at the Literary Colloquium Berlin.

34. In the foreword to the German edition, Arendt wrote, "This is not a word-for-word, literal translation of the English text. I had even written some chapters in German and later translated them into English; in these cases, I have restored their original titles here. But in addition, here and there I have made changes while reworking the text into

German—deletions and additions—that are not worth listing in detail here." *Elemente und Ursprünge totaler Herrschaft*, 15.

35. Nabokov, *Speak, Memory*, 9–10. At the "*Happy bin ich schon, aber glücklich bin ich nicht*" conference, Georg Witte drew attention to this quotation as well as to the children's songs and poems that Nabokov added to the Russian edition.

36. See the following chapter and the examples of comparative texts in the appendix; see also Hahn, *Hannah Arendt.*

37. *Ich will verstehen*, 4.

38. See the appendix. In his extremely valuable article "Arendt Against Athens: Rereading *The Human Condition*," Roy T. Tsao analyzes how the depictions of the Greeks diverge in the German and English versions of *The Human Condition.*

39. "I'm in the middle of translating the revolution book. I'm having fun, but I'm seeing again how difficult it is to transform something into another language. The better my English gets, the harder the German version is. Devil take this bilinguality!" Arendt/Jaspers *Correspondence*, letter of August 14, 1963. [There is no letter from this date in the English translation of the correspondence.—Trans.]

40. See Arendt's introduction to Benjamin, *Illuminations*, 24.

41. *Men in Dark Times*, 208.

42. Letter from J. Glenn Gray to Hannah Arendt, November 8, 1966, Library of Congress, Arendt Papers, Box 11.

43. Arendt/Jaspers, *Correspondence*, 173.

44. Benjamin, *Illuminations*, 255.

45. *On Revolution*, 284.

46. Arendt/Jaspers, *Correspondence*, 507. "In the course of your presentation," Jaspers wrote to Arendt, "the greatness to which you give expression is a source of encouragement" (505).

47. In *Between Past and Future*, 17–40.

48. Franz Kafka, *Die Romane* (Frankfurt: S. Fischer, 1965), 796.

49. *Responsibility and Judgment*, 259.

50. *New Yorker*, December 22, 1975.

FORGIVENESS

1. Berl Katznelson, "Talks to Youth," *Jewish Frontier* 9 (September 1945): 20–24; Arendt/Scholem, *Briefwechsel*, 127.

2. Katznelson, "Talks to Youth," 23.

3. Letter from Hannah Arendt to Dolf Sternberger, November 28, 1953, Deutsches Literaturarchiv, Marbach, Sternberger Nachlass.

4. Letter from Hannah Arendt to Dolf Sternberger, December 14, 1953, ibid. In her essay on Walter Benjamin, Arendt quotes from Heidegger's *Being and Time*, "The light of the public darkens everything." *Men in Dark Times*, 189.

5. For Arendt's use of the phrase "thinking without a banister," cf. *The Recovery of the Public World*, 336.

6. *Denktagebuch*, 300.

7. Ernst Grumach, a friend of her youth, survived the Nazi years as Oberjude (head Jew) in the Nazi organization Einsatzstab Reichsleiter Rosenberg, whose assignment was to expropriate Jewish cultural artifacts in the occupied territories.

8. Arendt/Jaspers, *Correspondence*, 54.

9. The Nazis knew that, Arendt wrote to Jaspers, and that's why they were so "*vergnügt*"(jolly or amused; "smug" in the English translation) at the Nuremberg trials. Ibid.

10. *Eichmann in Jerusalem*, 279.

11. *The Origins of Totalitarianism*, 459.

12. Letter from Hannah Arendt to Hugo Friedrich, July 15, 1953, Library of Congress, Hannah Arendt Archives, Box 10.

13. "Verstehen und Politik," *Zwischen Vergangenheit und Zukunft*, 125.

14. Deleuze, *Francis Bacon*, text volume, 55.

15. Jacob and Wilhelm Grimm, *Deutsches Wörterbuch* (1854), column 2529.

16. *The Human Condition*, 243.

17. Vladimir Jankélévitch, *Das Verzeihen, Essays zur Moral und Kulturphilosophie* (Frankfurt: Suhrkamp, 2003); Paul Ricoeur, *Das Rätsel der Vergangenheit. Erinnern, Vergessen, Verzeihen* (Göttingen: Wallstein, 1998).

18. In *Country of My Skull: Guilt, Sorrow, and the Limits of Forgiveness in the New South Africa* (New York: Broadway Books, 2000), her book on the Truth Commission, the Afrikaans writer Antjie Krog takes up Arendt's idea of forgiveness to conceive a new political confederation in postapartheid South Africa. See also Krog, "I speak holding up your heart": Cosmopolitanism, Forgiveness and Leaning towards Africa, Van der Leeuw Lecture, November 3, 2006. In *Stumme Gewalt: Nachdenken über die RAF* (Frankfurt: S. Fischer, 2010), the journalist Carolin Emcke deploys Arendt's conception of negotiated forgiveness to call for an end to the imprisonment of confessed RAF terrorists.

19. *Denktagebuch*, 1:7.

20. Ibid., 3.

21. Ibid.

22. Ibid.

23. "Of course, it's a different story if based on original sin. Then forgiveness is perhaps possible to the extent that it is only the explicit recognition that we are all sinners" (ibid., 4).

24. Nietzsche, *Also sprach Zarathustra*, 642.

25. *Denktagebuch*, 300.

26. See the extensive documentation in the biography by Young-Bruehl, *Hannah Arendt,* 287–90; see also the documents in the Library of

Congress, Hannah Arendt Papers, Box 57, from a course on the McCarthy era that Arendt gave at the University of Chicago in 1965.

27. *Essays in Understanding*, 400.

28. "You treat something that is, as though it were not and had to be realized in the future, hence, you begin to destroy it." Arendt's notes for the Whittaker Chambers–Alger Hiss seminar, 1965, Library of Congress, Hannah Arendt Papers, Box 57.

29. Both quotes from *The Human Condition*, 237.

30. Arendt and McCarthy, *Between Friends*, 6.

31. As Arendt warned, "The end of a tradition does not necessarily mean that traditional concepts have lost their power over the minds of men. On the contrary, it sometimes seems that this power of well-worn notions and categories becomes more tyrannical as the tradition loses its living force and as the memory of its beginning recedes. *Between Past and Future*, 25–26.

32. "Here Smith conforms to Jones and Jones conforms to Smith," letter from Hannah Arendt to Dolf Sternberger, November 28, 1953, Deutsche Literaturarchiv Marbach, Sternberger Nachlass.

33. Letter of August 16, 1953, Arendt/Scholem, *Briefwechsel,* 385.

34. Alfred Kazin, *New York Jew* (New York: Knopf, 1978), 203.

35. *The Origins of Totalitarianism*, 345.

36. See Hahn and Knott, *Hannah Arendt*.

37. In "Thinking and Moral Considerations," she writes of Adolf Eichmann, "To his rather limited supply of stock phrases he had added a few new ones, and he was utterly helpless only when he was confronted with a situation to which none of them would apply, as in the most grotesque instance when he had to make a speech under the gallows and was forced to rely on clichés used in funeral oratory which were inapplicable in his case because he was not the survivor. Considering what his last words should be in case of the death sentence, which he had expected

all along, the simple fact had not occurred to him, just as inconsistencies and flagrant contradictions in examination and cross-examinations during the trial had not bothered him. Clichés, stock phrases, adherence to conventional, standardized codes of expression and conduct have the socially recognized function of protecting us against reality, that is, against the claim on our thinking attention which all events and facts arouse by virtue of their existence. If we were responsive to this claim all the time, we would soon be exhausted; the difference in Eichmann was only that he clearly knew of no such claim at all." *Responsibility and Judgment*, 160.

38. *The Origins of Totalitarianism*, 474.

39. *Denktagebuch*, 1:11.

40. Ibid., 312.

41. Hannah Arendt, "Karl Marx," Part III, 23, quoted in *Was ist Politik?*, 226.

42. *Essays in Understanding*, 399.

43. *Denktagebuch*, 1:14, n912. In *Thus Spake Zarathustra*, Nietzsche wrote, "The promise life makes to us, we will—keep it to life!"

44. *Denktagebuch*, 1:9.

45. Ibid., 135, quoting Nietzsche.

46. *The Human Condition*, 247.

47. Reichert, *Die unendliche Aufgabe*, 169–70.

48. *The Human Condition*, 238.

49. Ibid., 239–40.

50. Ibid., 240, n78.

51. "Without being forgiven, released from the consequences of what we have done, our capacity to act would, as it were, be confined to one single deed from which we could never recover; we would remain the victims of its consequences forever." *The Human Condition*, 237.

52. Ibid., 240.

53. Auden took special notice of Arendt's discussion of forgiveness in his review of the book, which he said he had been waiting for all his life: "Action tends to be as boundless as the freedom in which it is grounded and would destroy us, if we would not set limits to what we do." The self-imposed limits Auden has in mind correspond to Arendt's "reliable places" for action: laws, forgiveness, promising. Auden, "Thinking What We Are Doing," 72–76. Instead of writing an autobiography, Auden collected sayings, figures of speech, and thoughts in *A Certain World: A Commonplace Book* (New York: Viking, 1970). They constituted the building in which his thought dwelled—he called it the landscape of his dreams, the basic atmosphere in which his imagination developed. Some entries were simply for pleasure. With others, he hoped to unsettle the reader as much as he was unsettled himself. Among the latter there is a quotation about forgiveness from *The Human Condition*. Forgiveness is "the only reaction that acts in an unexpected way and thus retains, though being a reaction, something of the original character of action."

54. Auden, "The Fallen City."

55. Letter from Hannah Arendt to W. H. Auden, February 14, 1960, Hannah Arendt Papers, Library of Congress.

56. *The Human Condition*, 243. The German version: "If there were no fellow human beings, we could not forgive ourselves any failing or transgression because closed within ourselves, we would lack the person who is more than the wrong he has committed."

57. Letter from Benno von Wiese to Hannah Arendt, October 17, 1953, Deutsches Literaturarchiv, Marbach am Neckar.

58. Benno von Wiese, "Bemerkungen zur unbewältigten Vergangenheit" (Remarks on the unmastered past), *Die Zeit*, December 25, 1964.

59. Letter from Hannah Arendt to Benno von Wiese, December 25, 1964, in Rossade, "'Dem Zeitgeist erlegen,'" 179ff.

60. Letter from Hannah Arendt to Benno von Wiese, February 19, 1965, ibid., 183.

61. See *The Life of the Mind*, 1:173.

DRAMATIZATION

1. Auden, "The Fallen City," 28.

2. *The Human Condition*, 179. In *Vita activa*, Arendt's German translation of *The Human Condition*, the last clause is rendered as "[sie] treten gleichsam auf die Bühne der Welt"—as if stepping onto the stage of the world (167).

3. *The Human Condition*, 198; in the corresponding passage in *Vita activa*, she writes, "Der politische Bereich im Sinne der Griechen gleicht einer solchen immerwährenden Bühne, auf der es gewissermaßen nur ein Auftreten, aber kein Abtreten gibt"—The political realm in the sense of the Greeks resembles such an eternal stage, where there is as it were only an entrance and never an exit (249).

4. *The Life of the Mind*, 1:207.

5. This chapter is based on works on intertextuality and performativity, especially those of Mieke Bal, Erika Fischer-Lichte, Dieter Mersch, Wolfgang Iser, and Klaus Reichert.

6. Rainer Maria Rilke, Ninth Duino Elegy, *Sämtliche Werke* (Frankfurt: Insel Verlag, 1975), 2:717.

7. "Rilkes Duineser Elegien."

8. In German, "die Bretter, die die Welt bedeuten," a line from Friedrich Schiller's poem "An die Freunde" (To my friends) that has become a figure of speech equivalent to "All the world's a stage" in English. —Trans.

9. See *The Human Condition*, 173.

10. Rilke, Seventh Duino Elegy, 2:711.

11. *Denktagebuch*, 118.

12. Ibid.; Martin Heidegger, *Gesamtausgabe* (Frankfurt: Kostermann, 1976–2011), 9:313–64.

13. *The Life of the Mind*, 1:75.

14. Peter Sloterdijk, *Du musst dein Leben ändern* (Frankfurt: Suhrkamp, 2009).

15. *Denktagebuch*, 1:9.

16. Benjamin, *Illuminations*, 261.

17. *Vita activa*, 248–49.

18. *Zur Zeit*, 184.

19. *Essays in Understanding*, 74.

20. See Ingeborg Nordmann, "Gedankenexperiment und Zitatmontage," in Heuer and von der Lühe, *Dichterisch Denken*, 162–86.

21. See Rosenzweig, "Nachwort zu den Hymnen und Gedichten des Jehuda Halevi," 210. In his essay on Rosenzweig and Buber's Bible translation, Reichert writes that Rosenzweig called such intertextuality "mosaic style" and said that it was well-known in Hebrew. "The Jew in the Middle Ages," Reichert continues, "was so familiar with the classical texts and especially the Bible and at the same time so sure of his style that it was all the same to him whether he quoted or spoke in his own name; quotation had become so much a part of his own thoughts and feelings that it never functioned as a reference to an authority or as mere ornament." *Die unendliche Aufgabe*, 163.

22. *Men in Dark Times*, 197, quoting Benjamin, *Gesammelte Schriften* I, 416.

23. Friedrich Nietzsche, *Nachlass*, Fall 1881, Fragmente 11, *Sämtliche Werke: Kritische Studienausgabe* (Munich: Deutscher Taschenbuch Verlag, 1999), 9:119. The quotation continues: "...then the struggle is within him, and he must put all his powers at the disposal of the individual phantasma, and later of another one."

24. *The Human Condition*, 169–70.

25. Ibid., 170.

26. *Vita activa*, 212, translated by David Dollenmayer. "Eloquent in word and vigorous in deed" (*beredt in Worten und rüstig in Taten*) is from Johann Heinrich Voss's translation of Homer's *Iliad*, Book 28, line 443; "all the glory of man as the flower of grass" is from I Peter, 1:24. Compare the quite different passage in *The Human Condition*, 173–74, which does not include the biblical reference. On this passage, see also Hahn, *Hannah Arendt*.

27. I Peter 1:24–25.

28. Karl Jaspers discussed these lines extensively in *Von der Wahrheit*, and Arendt wrote him after reading it, "It is a great book," especially "the pages on *Hamlet*." Arendt/Jaspers, *Correspondence*, 148.

29. *The Jewish Writings*, 295.

30. *Essays in Understanding*, 444–45.

31. Ibid., 435, 438.

32. *The Promise of Politics*, 203.

33. Ibid., 201.

34. From Fontane's ballad "Die Brück' am Tay" (The Bridge on the Tay) about a train wreck on the bridge across the Firth of Tay in Scotland on December 30, 1879.—Trans.

35. *Was ist Politik?*, Fragment 4, 182.

36. On the "two-in-one" of thinking, see Arendt's comments in "Some Questions of Moral Philosophy," in *Responsibility and Judgment*, 184–85, and *The Life of the Mind*, 1:179–93.

37. On "per-sonare" as "durchtönen" (sounding through), see the typescript of the Sonning Prize speech at the Library of Congress, http://memory.loc.gov/cgi-bin/ampage?collid=mharendt&fileName=05/052270/052270page.db&recNum=0.

38. *Vita activa*, chap. 24, 220. This sentence is not included in *The Human Condition*, chap. 24, 180.

39. *Men in Dark Times*, 25.

40. See my remarks on Paul Valéry and Nathalie Sarraute in Hahn and Knott, *Hannah Arendt*, 151–55.

41. Arendt and McCarthy, *Between Friends*, 241.

42. See Tatjana Tömmel's entry on friendship in Heuer, Heiter, and Rosenmüller, *Arendt-Handbuch*.

43. *Men in Dark Times*, 193.

44. Arendt/Jaspers, *Correspondence*, 200.

45. *The Life of the Mind*, 1:47.

46. See Helmut Lachenmann, "Hören ist wehrlos — ohne Hören," in *Musik als existentielle Erfahrung* (Frankfurt: Suhrkamp, 1996), 118.

47. *Essays in Understanding*, 183.

48. Reichert, *Die unendliche Aufgabe*, 163.

49. As she wrote of Kafka, "He wanted to build up a world in accordance with human needs and human dignities, a world where man's actions are determined by himself and which is ruled by his laws and not by mysterious forces emanating from above or from below." *Essays in Understanding*, 80.

50. Letter from Hannah Arendt to Hugo Friedrich, July 15, 1953, Library of Congress, Box 10.

51. Ibid.

52. Concerning the opposite stylistic device, the cultural critic Mieke Bal writes, "When someone makes a verb into a noun, the concept becomes amenable to analysis and discussion. That is a gain. But there are also losses. One loses sight of the active aspect of the referent, the narrational aspect of the action including the subjectivity of the participants. *If the subject of the action disappears, so does the responsibility for the action.*" *Kulturanalyse*, 56.

53. *On Revolution*, 237–38.

54. *Über die Revolution*, 301ff.

55. Arendt/Broch, *Briefwechsel*, 175.

56. *The Life of the Mind*, 1:94.

APPENDIX

1. The (sometimes imprecise) quotations are from a late poem draft by Rilke, "Komm du, du letzter, den ich anerkenne," in Rilke, *Sämtliche Werke*, 3:511.—Trans.

2. Quoted in Hahn and Knott, *Hannah Arendt*, 188.

3. See the epigraph to Chapter Two above (page 31) and its note.

BIBLIOGRAPHY

WORKS BY HANNAH ARENDT

Between Past and Future: Eight Exercises in Political Thought. Edited by Jerome Kohn. New York: Penguin, 2006.

Denktagebuch 1950–1973. 2 vols. Edited by Ursula Ludz and Ingeborg Nordmann. Munich: Piper, 2002.

Eichmann in Jerusalem: A Report on the Banality of Evil. Introduction by Amos Elon. New York: Penguin, 2006.

Eichmann in Jerusalem: Ein Bericht von der Banalität des Bösen. Hamburg: Rowohlt, 1978.

Elemente und Ursprünge totaler Herrschaft. Munich: Piper, 2005.

Essays in Understanding, 1930–1954. Edited by Jerome Kohn. New York: Harcourt, 1994.

The Human Condition. Chicago: University of Chicago Press, 1958.

Ich will verstehen: Selbstauskünfte zu Leben und Werk. Edited by Ursula Ludz. Munich: Piper, 1997.

The Jew as Pariah: Jewish Identity and Politics in the Modern Age. Edited by Ron H. Feldman. New York: Grove Press, 1978.

The Jewish Writings. Edited by Jerome Kohn and Ron H. Feldman. New York: Schocken Books, 2007.

The Life of the Mind. Vol. 1, *Thinking*; Vol. 2, *Willing.* Edited by Mary McCarthy. New York: Harcourt, 1977.

Men in Dark Times. New York: Harcourt, 1968.

"Nathalie Sarraute." *New York Review of Books*, March 5, 1964, 5–6.

On Revolution. New York: Viking, 1963.

The Origins of Totalitarianism. New edition with added prefaces. New York: Harcourt, 1973.

The Promise of Politics. Edited by Jerome Kohn. New York: Schocken Books, 2005.

The Recovery of the Public World. Edited by Melvyn Hill. New York: St. Martin's Press, 1979.

Responsibility and Judgment. Edited by Jerome Kohn. New York: Schocken Books, 2003.

"Rilkes Duineser Elegien." *Neue Schweizer Rundschau* 23, no. 11 (1930): 855–71 (co-author Gunther Stern).

Sechs Essays. Heidelberg: L. Schneider, 1948.

Über das Böse: Eine Vorlesung zu Fragen der Ethik. Edited by Jerome Kohn. Munich: Piper, 2006.

Über die Revolution. Munich: Piper, 1974.

Vita activa oder Vom tätigen Leben. Munich: Piper, 2002.

Was ist Politik? Fragmente aus dem Nachlass. Edited by Ursula Ludz. Munich: Piper, 1993.

Zur Zeit: Politische Essays. Edited by Marie Luise Knott. Berlin: Rotbuch Verlag, 1986.

Zwischen Vergangenheit und Zukunft. Munich: Piper, 1994.

CORRESPONDENCE

Arendt, Hannah, and Heinrich Blücher. *Within Four Walls: The Correspondence Between Hannah Arendt and Heinrich Blücher, 1936–1968*. Edited by Lotte Kohler. Translated by Peter Constantine. New York: Harcourt, 2000.

Arendt, Hannah, and Hermann Broch. *Briefwechsel, 1946–1951*. Edited by Paul Michael Lützeler. Frankfurt: Suhrkamp, 1996.

Arendt, Hannah, and Martin Heidegger. *Letters, 1925–1975.* Edited by Ursula Ludz. Translated by Andrew Shields. New York: Harcourt, 2004.

Arendt, Hannah, and Karl Jaspers. *Correspondence, 1926–1969.* Translated by Robert and Rita Kimber. New York: Harcourt, 1992.

Arendt, Hannah, and Mary McCarthy. *Between Friends: The Correspondence of Hannah Arendt and Mary McCarthy, 1949–1975.* Edited by Carol Brightman. New York: Harcourt, 1995.

Arendt, Hannah, and Gershom Scholem. *Der Briefwechsel, 1939–1964.* Edited by Marie Luise Knott. Berlin: Jüdischer Verlag, 2010.

SECONDARY LITERATURE

Améry, Jean. "Das Leben zwischen den Sprachen." *Die Zeit*, September 3, 1976.

Auden, W. H. "The Fallen City: Some Reflections on Shakespeare's *Henry IV*." *Encounter* 74 (November 1959): 21–34. www.unz.org/Pub/Encounter-1959nov-00021.

———. "Thinking What We Are Doing." *Encounter* 69 (June 1959): 72–76.

Bal, Mieke. *Kulturanalyse.* Frankfurt: Suhrkamp, 2002.

Baumgart, Reinhard. "Mit Mördern leben." *Merkur* 206 (1965): 482ff.

Benjamin, Walter. "Der Autor als Produzent." *Gesammelte Schriften* II/2. Frankfurt: Suhrkamp, 1972–89, 699.

———. *Illuminations: Essays and Reflections.* Edited and with an introduction by Hannah Arendt. Translated by Harry Zohn. New York: Harcourt, 1968.

Blumenberg, Hans. *Zu den Sachen und zurück.* Frankfurt: Suhrkamp, 2002.

Brauer, Gerhard. *The Problem with Reading Hannah Arendt in English.* Stuttgart: VDM Verlag, 2011.

Deleuze, Gilles. *Francis Bacon—Logik der Sensation.* Translated by Joseph Vogel. Munich: Wilhelm Fink, 1995.

Elon, Amos. "The Excommunication of Hannah Arendt." Introduction to *Eichmann in Jerusalem*, vii–xxiii.

Fest, Joachim. "Hannah Arendt im Gespräch mit Joachim Fest: Eine Rundfunksendung aus dem Jahr 1964." Edited by Ursula Ludz and Thomas Wild. www.hannaharendt.net/index.php/han/article/view/114/194.

Hahn, Barbara. *Hannah Arendt—Leidenschaften, Menschen und Bücher*. Berlin: Berlin Verlag, 2005.

Hahn, Barbara, and Marie Luise Knott. *Hannah Arendt—Von den Dichtern erwarten wir Wahrheit*. Berlin: Matthes & Seitz, 2007.

Heuer, Wolfgang, Bernd Heiter, and Stefanie Rosenmüller, eds. *Arendt-Handbuch:Leben, Werk, Wirkung*. Stuttgart: J.B. Metzler, 2011.

Heuer, Wolfgang, and I. von der Lühe, eds. *Dichterisch Denken: Hannah Arendt und die Künste*. Göttingen: Wallstein, 2007.

Iser, Wolfgang. "Das Spiel im Spiel: Formen dramatischer Illusion bei Shakespeare." *Archiv für das Studium der neueren Sprachen* 198 (1961): 209–26.

Jaspers, Karl. *Von der Wahrheit*. Munich: Piper, 1947.

Mersch, Dieter. *Ereignis und Aura*. Frankfurt: Suhrkamp, 2002.

Nabokov, Vladimir. *Speak, Memory: An Autobiography Revisited*. New York: Putnam, 1966.

Nietzsche, Friedrich. *Also sprach Zarathustra*, in *Werke in zwei Bänden*. Munich: Carl Hanser, 1967, 1:545–778.

Plessner, Helmuth. *Lachen und Weinen. Eine Untersuchung nach den Grenzen des menschlichen Verhaltens*. Arnhem: Van Loghum Slaterus, 1941.

Reichert, Klaus. *Die unendliche Aufgabe: Zum Übersetzen*. Munich: Hanser, 2006.

Rosenzweig, Franz. "Nachwort zu den Hymnen und Gedichten des Jehuda Halevi," in *Kleinere Schriften*. Berlin: Schocken, 1932, 200–19.

Rossade, Klaus-Dieter. *"Dem Zeitgeist erlegen": Benno von Wiese und der Nationalsozialismus*. Heidelberg: Synchron, 2007.

Schiller, Friedrich. *Sämtliche Werke*. Vol. 1, *Gedichte, Dramen I*. Darmstadt: Wissenschaftliche Buchgesellschaft, 1987.

Tsao, Roy T. "Arendt Against Athens: Rereading *The Human Condition*." *Political Theory* 30, no. 1 (February 2002): 97–123.

Young-Bruehl, Elisabeth. *Hannah Arendt: For Love of the World*. New Haven: Yale University Press, 1982.

KEY TO THE ILLUSTRATIONS

LAUGHTER, P. 2

Blatt = leaf; piece of paper

Frieden = peace

Kein Blatt vor den Mund nehmen (literally, "Not putting a leaf in front of one's mouth") = Not mincing words.

Blatt auf Blatt = leaf after leaf *or* leaf on page

Blätter = leaves

blättern = to page *or* leaf through (a book)

lesen = to read

Zeit = time

Ast = branch

Knast = (slang) jail, the clink, the pen

Zaun = fence

Grenze = border

Teilung = division; sharing

Beispiel für eine ungerechte (Teilung) = example of an unfair division

Ende = end

nah = near

fern = far, distant

hier = here

Vorstellung = idea, notion

    kann was = can do something

    Leinwand = canvas

    Einwand = objection, dissent

    Einwanderung = immigration

    Grat = mountain ridge (*Gratwanderung* = balancing act)

    übersetzen = to carry across; translate

Not = emergency

Exil = exile

lieber Tee = rather have tea

    (*Tee* is pronounced "tay," which is also how one says

    the letter T)

2 Striche = 2 lines

3 Striche = 3 lines

Anfang = beginning

Hut = hat

hat = has

Mut = courage

Mut haben = having courage

sein = to be; being

nicht sein = not being

Sein und Zeit = "Being and Time"
  (the title of Martin Heidegger's magnum opus)

schwarz = black

weiss = white

Dichter = poet

Nebel = fog, mist

  Wolke = cloud

  Gedanke = thought → *danke* = thank you

    Einfall = idea   *bitte* = you're welcome

    ein Fall = a fall   *keine Ursache* = no need
                            (to thank me); no cause

                          kein Grund = no cause *or*
                            reason; no ground

Sprache = speech, language

Ach und Weh = groaning and lamentation
  (*weh* is pronounced "vay," which is also how one says
  the letter W, hence *www*)

wo = where

Heimat = homeland

Heim = home

anfangen = to begin

left-hand sequence:

    Poesie = poetry

    Band = ribbon; volume

    Einband = [book] binding

    Werke = works

    dies = this

    das = that

    Mensch = human being; man!

    Mensch, ärgere dich nicht! = Man, don't get annoyed!

        (name of a popular board game)

right-hand sequences:

    valsch (misspelling of) *falsch* = rong (misspelling of) wrong

    Zeit = time

    Raum = space; room

        Erde = earth

        Hoffnung = hope

        Wunsch = wish

        Wirklichkeit = reality

    Lebensraum = "room for living"

        (policy of German expansionism in Eastern Europe)

    Bretter = boards (also a metaphor for the stage)

    ein Brett vor dem Kopf haben (literally, "to have a board in front

        of one's head") = to be a blockhead

    Bretter, die die Welt bedeuten = "boards that signify the world"

        (Friedrich Schiller)

APPENDIX, P. 114

valsch (misspelling of) *falsch* = rong (misspelling of) wrong
Poesie = poetry
Sie = you (formal)
du = you (familiar)
den = him (accusative case)
dem = to *or* for him (dative case)
der = he *or* the (masculine, nominative case)
er = he
die Überschrift = caption, heading
die Unterschrift = signature

MARIE LUISE KNOTT is a journalist, translator, and author. She founded the German edition of *Le Monde diplomatique* in 1995 and has been its editor-in-chief for eleven years. She writes on art and literature and has edited several books of Hannah Arendt's writings, including the correspondence between Arendt and Gershom Scholem (Chicago University Press, 2014). In 2012 Knott coedited and translated *Empty Mind*, the poetic writings of John Cage. She lives in Berlin.

DAVID DOLLENMAYER is a literary translator and emeritus professor of German at Worcester Polytechnic Institute in Massachusetts. His translations include works by Bertolt Brecht, Elias Canetti, Peter Stephan Jungk, Michael Kleeberg, Michael Köhlmeier, Perikles Monioudis, Anna Mitgutsch, Mietek Pemper, Moses Rosenkranz, and Hansjörg Schertenleib. He is the recipient of the 2008 Helen and Kurt Wolff Translator's Prize and the 2010 Translation Prize of the Austrian Cultural Forum in New York.